SUSCEPTIBLE

by geneviève castrée

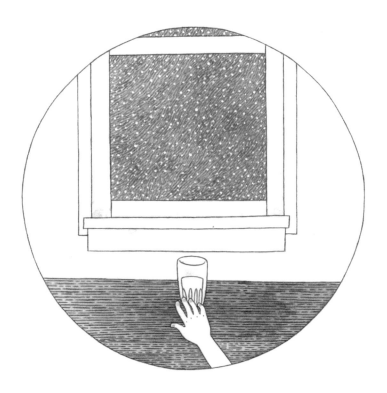

drawn & quarterly

MONTRÉAL

Drawn & Quarterly
Post Office Box 48056
Montréal, Québec
Canada H2V 4S8
www.drawnandquarterly.com

First hardcover edition: September 2012
Printed by Friesens in Altona, Manitoba, Canada.

10 9 8 7 6 5 4 3 2 1

Library and Archives Canada Cataloguing in Publication
Castrée, Geneviève, 1981–
Susceptible / Geneviève Castrée.
ISBN 978-1-77046-088-1
1. Graphic Novels. I. Title.
PN6733.C3898S98 2012   741.5'971 C2012-902517-8

The author wishes to thank Canada Council for the Arts for the help provided.

Drawn & Quarterly acknowledges the financial support of the Government of Canada through the Canada Book Fund and the Canada Council for the Arts for our publishing activities and for the support of this edition.

Distributed in the U.S.A. by:
Farrar, Strauss and Giroux
18 West 18th Street
New York, NY 10011
Orders: 888.330.8477

Distributed in Canada by:
Raincoast Books
2440 Viking Way
Richmond · BC
V6V 1N2
Orders: 800.663.5714

" but blood does bring curiosity. "

- JOANNE KYGER
(from the poem
    "My father died this spring")

I often think
about what is innate
and what is acquired.

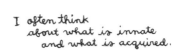

are our genes
ever a valid
excuse?

I wonder if it is possible
for a sadness to be
passed from one
generation to the other...

... if my depressions could be
caused by emotions accumulated by me,
but also by my parents, my
ancestors even.

or if those difficult moments
are simply provoked by
what falls onto me.

Maybe it is just my
core that is rotten...

... maybe my internal fauna
and flora are too fragile,
unbalanced.

AAAAARRGHH!

That is possible.

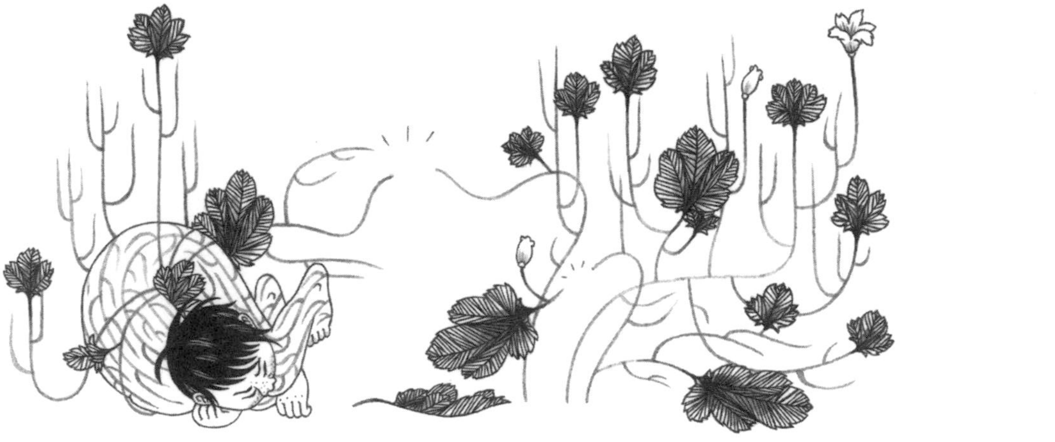

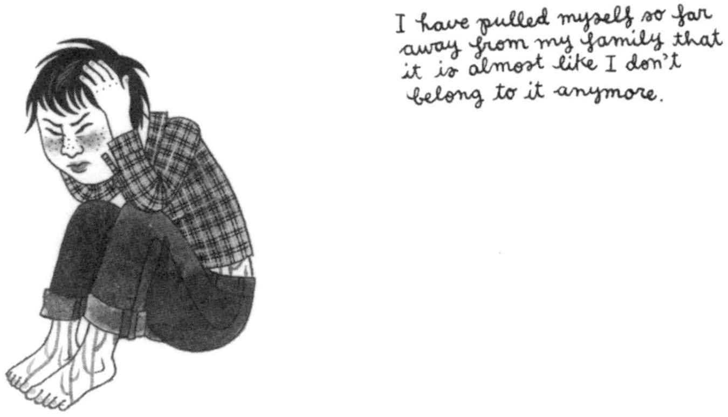
I have pulled myself so far away from my family that it is almost like I don't belong to it anymore.

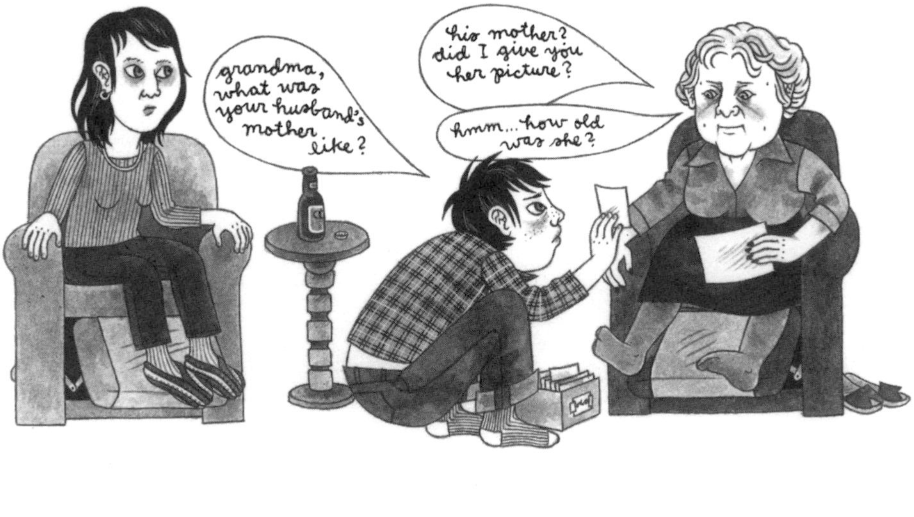
grandma, what was your husband's mother like?
his mother? did I give you her picture?
hmm... how old was she?

My mother is the youngest of a family of sixteen children. Her father died when she was still very young. I ask my grandmother to tell me about my great-grandmother, a first nations woman. Most people from Québec have some aboriginal blood, it is not very exotic.

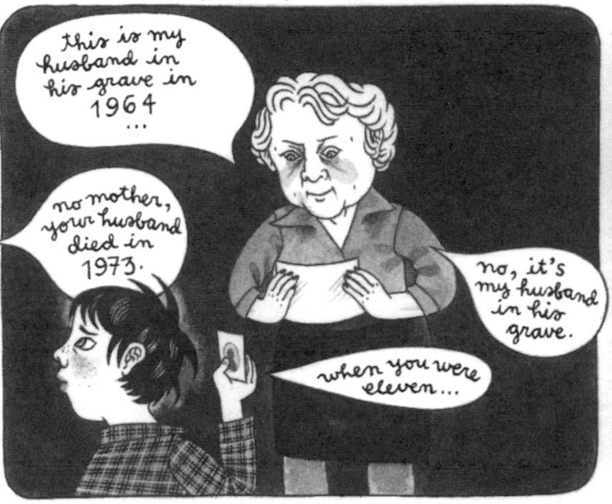
this is my husband in his grave in 1964 ...
no mother, your husband died in 1973.
no, it's my husband in his grave.
when you were eleven...

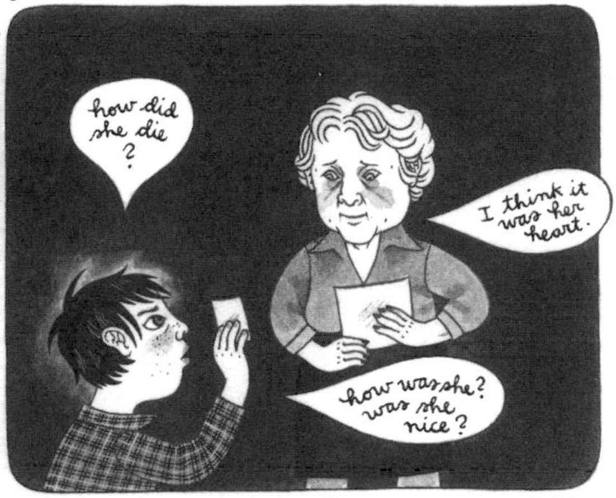
how did she die ?
I think it was her heart.
how was she? was she nice?

My grandmother lives alone. She is very old, very happy, and very Catholic. Once, I was told that after having her first thirteen children she took a little break for three years until her village priest told her to get on with her "duty as a woman" while she was still good.

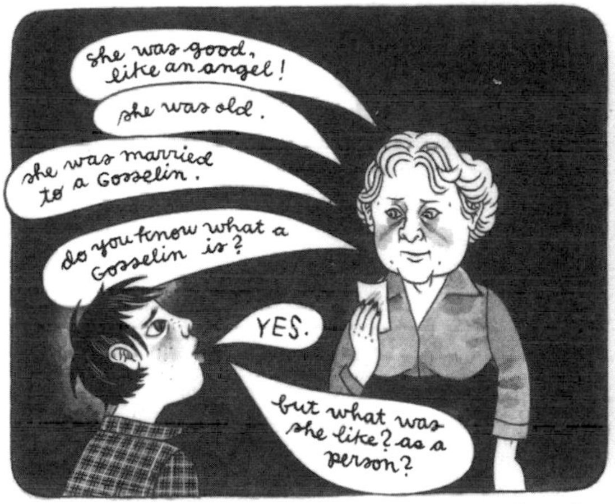
she was good, like an angel!
she was old.
she was married to a Gosselin.
do you know what a Gosselin is?
YES.
but what was she like? as a person?

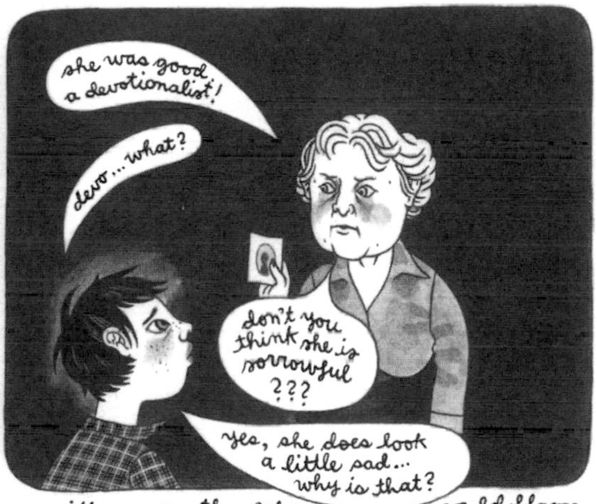
she was good a devotionalist!
devo...what?
don't you think she is sorrowful ???
yes, she does look a little sad... why is that?

My grandmother forgets our names and confuses us with one another. Who could blame her? I would have trouble writing the list of all my aunts, uncles, girl and boy cousins and their children... Some of them I have never met. As a family, you can know one another poorly.

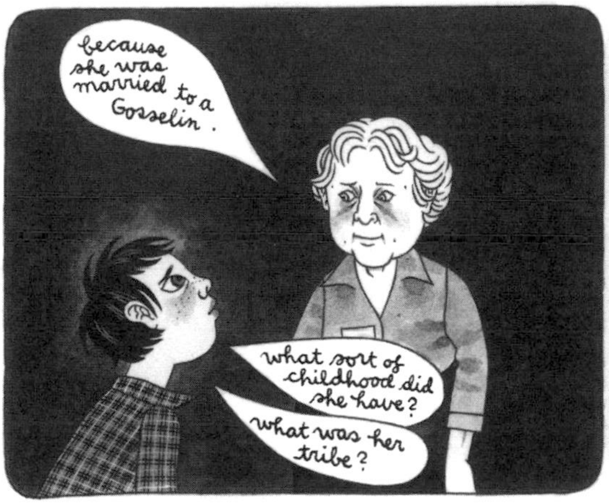
because she was married to a Gosselin.
what sort of childhood did she have?
what was her tribe?

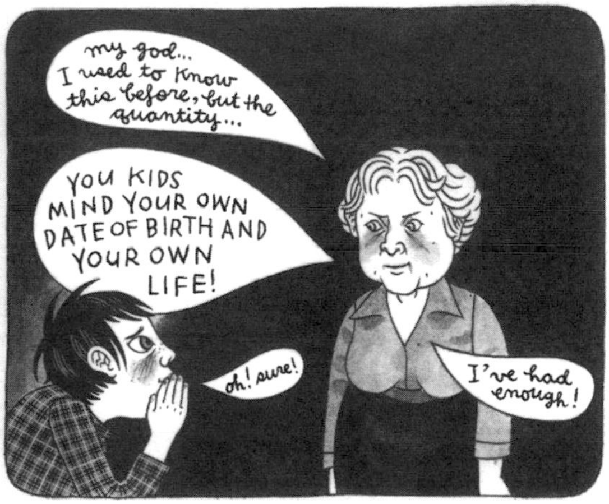
my god... I used to know this before, but the quantity...
YOU KIDS MIND YOUR OWN DATE OF BIRTH AND YOUR OWN LIFE!
oh! sure!
I've had enough!

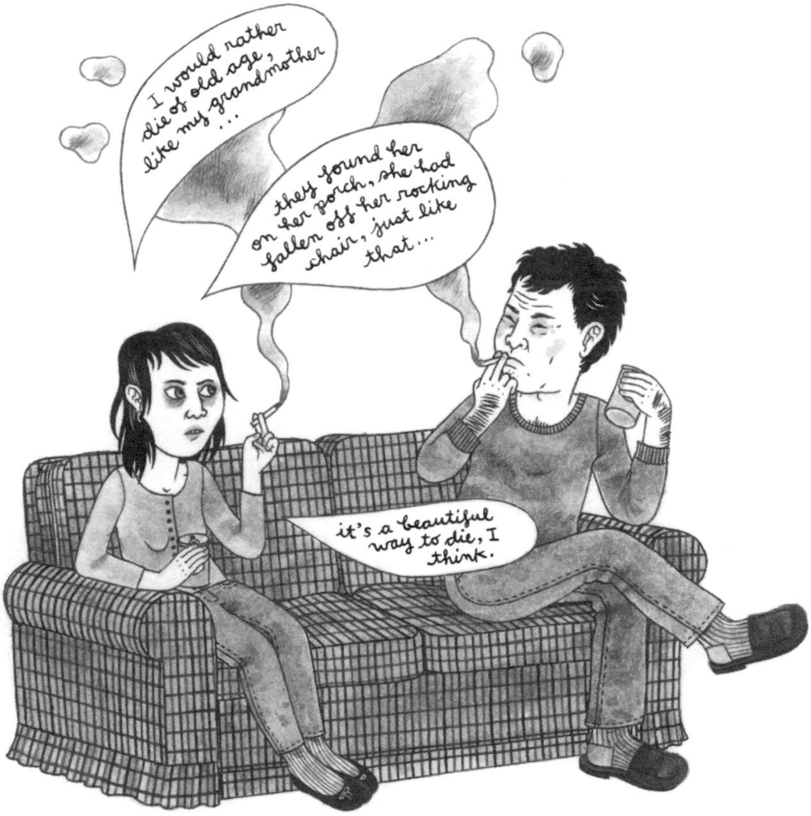
I would rather die of old age, like my grandmother ...
they found her on her porch, she had fallen off her rocking chair, just like that...
it's a beautiful way to die, I think.

Amère is my mother. Amer is her boyfriend. I listen to them talk when I finish my supper.

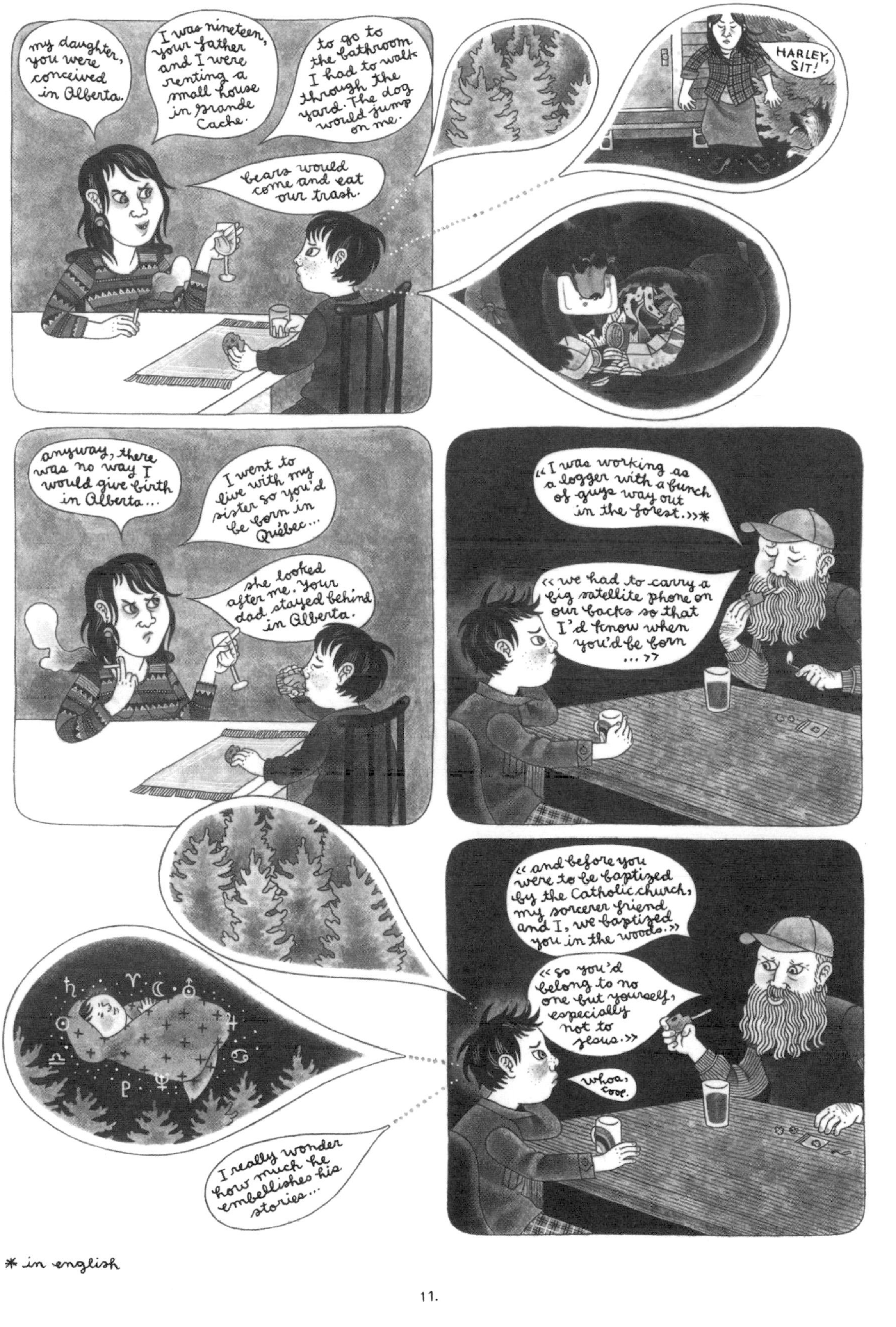
my daughter, you were conceived in Alberta.
I was nineteen, your father and I were renting a small house in Grande Cache.
to go to the bathroom I had to walk through the yard. The dog would jump on me.
HARLEY, SIT!
bears would come and eat our trash.
anyway, there was no way I would give birth in Alberta...
I went to live with my sister so you'd be born in Québec...
she looked after me. Your dad stayed behind in Alberta.
« I was working as a logger with a bunch of guys way out in the forest. »*
« we had to carry a big satellite phone on our backs so that I'd know when you'd be born ... »
« and before you were to be baptized by the Catholic church, my sorcerer friend and I, we baptized you in the woods. »
« so you'd belong to no one but yourself, especially not to Jesus. »
Whoa, cool.
I really wonder how much he embellishes his stories...

* in english

Tête d'Oeuf, my father, does not speak French. One time before I was born, two of my uncles made him repeat silly stuff: "je suis une tête d'oeuf" (I am an egg head) to make everyone laugh. My father left us many times. I vaguely remember his "real" departure.

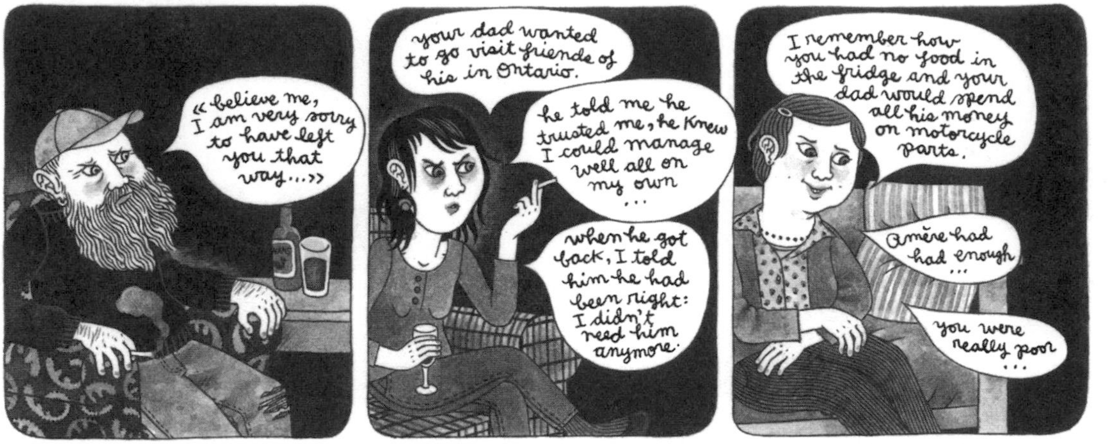

« believe me, I am very sorry to have left you that way...»
your dad wanted to go visit friends of his in Ontario.
he told me he trusted me, he knew I could manage well all on my own ...
when he got back, I told him he had been right: I didn't need him anymore.
I remember how you had no food in the fridge and your dad would spend all his money on motorcycle parts.
Amère had had enough ...
you were really poor ...

I am two years old. Amère, Tête d'Oeuf and I live on the second (maybe third) floor. An autumn night, it is raining. I am looking at my father from the window. He is getting ready to climb on his motorcycle. I have little plastic guys on the tips of my fingers.

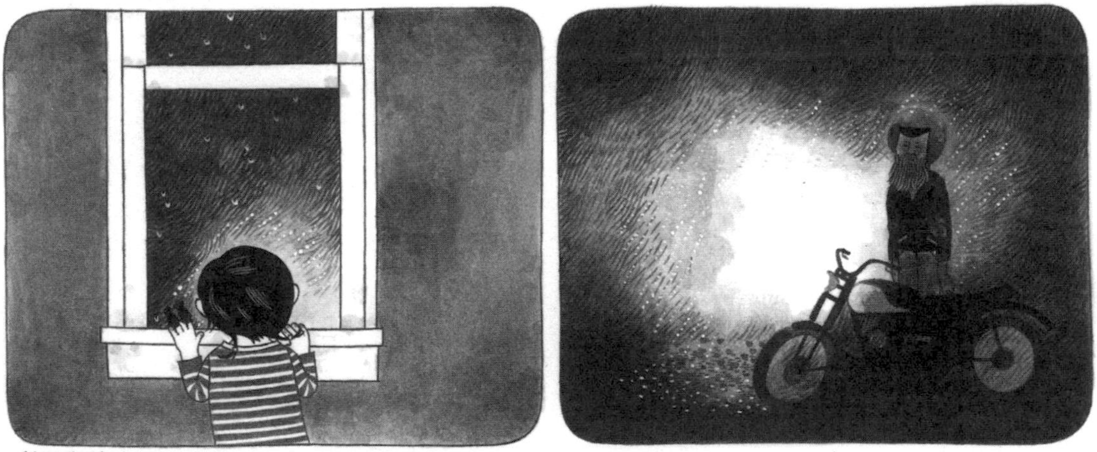

My father is waiting for somebody. There is sadness in the air. In my mind everything is so slow. My father is getting soaking wet in the dark while the water is glistening around the asphalt and the dead leaves. He is only lit up by his motorcycle's headlight.

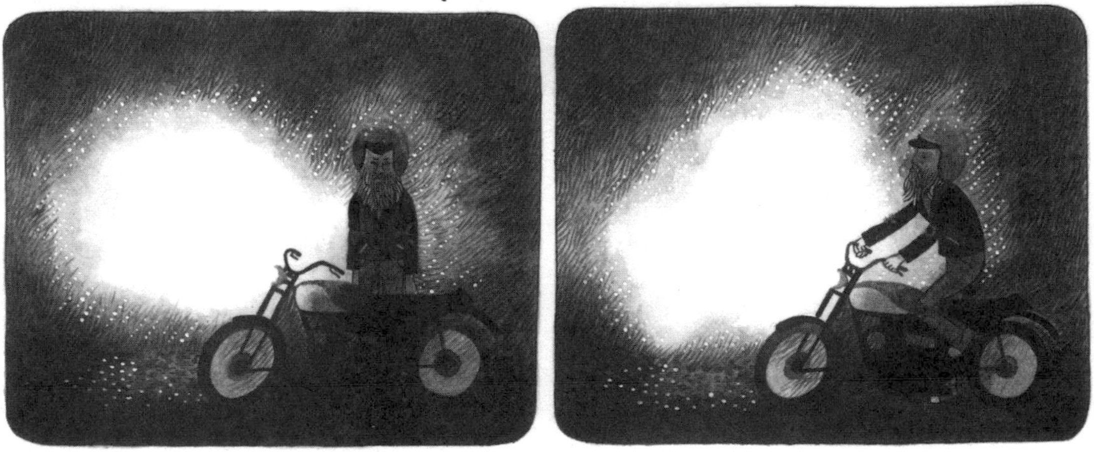

I can hear the sound of a motor, and then another motor getting closer. Tête d'Oeuf's cars and motorcycles tend to be fragile and require a lot of fixing. He insists on doing it all by himself. He prefers what is old, what has character, even if it is broken.

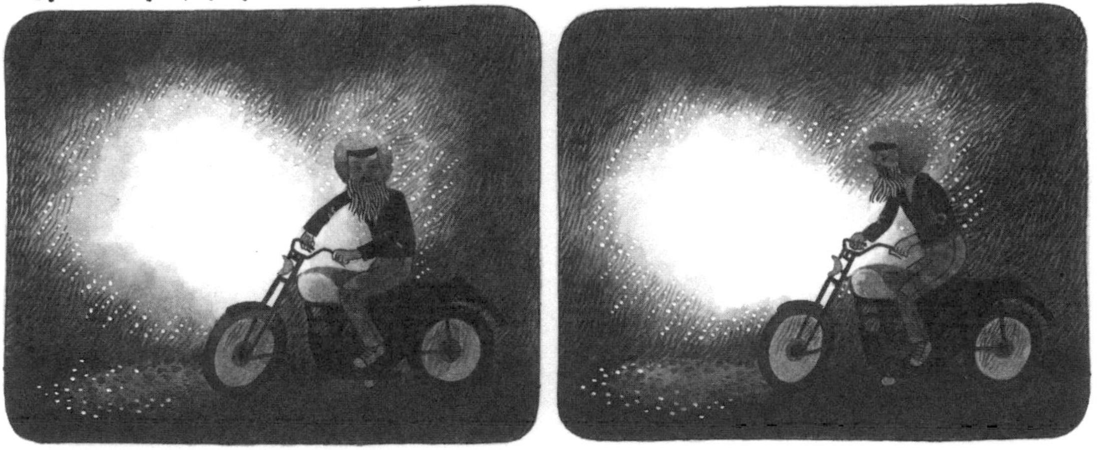

My father is met by a friend on another bike. He is a man with brown hair and a moustache. I know him. I went to his house once, he played me a record of meteorological sounds, thunder. His little black dog bit me.

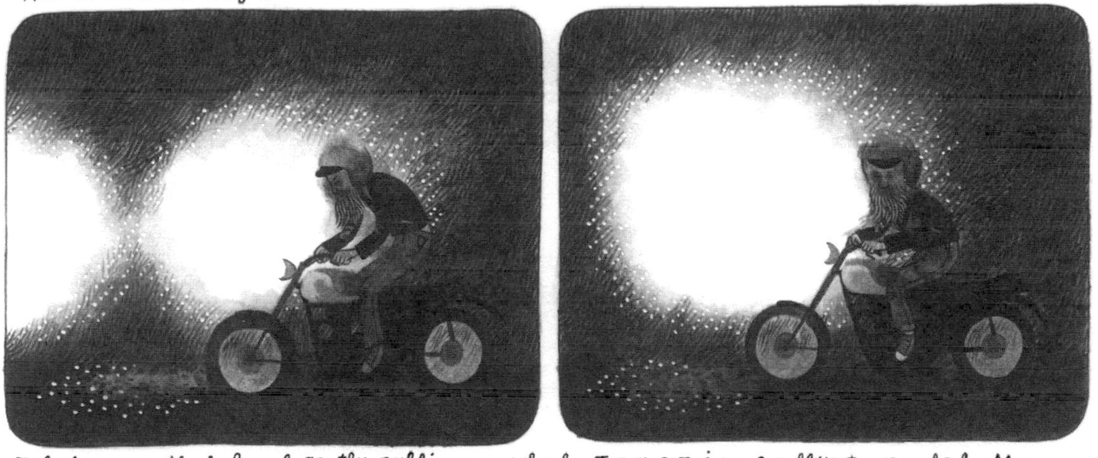

I feel my mother's hand gently rubbing my back. I am waving goodbye to my dad. My mother raises me alone. That is why I can't speak English. Tête d'Oeuf disappears and reappears once in a while. I change tremendously in between each of his appearances.

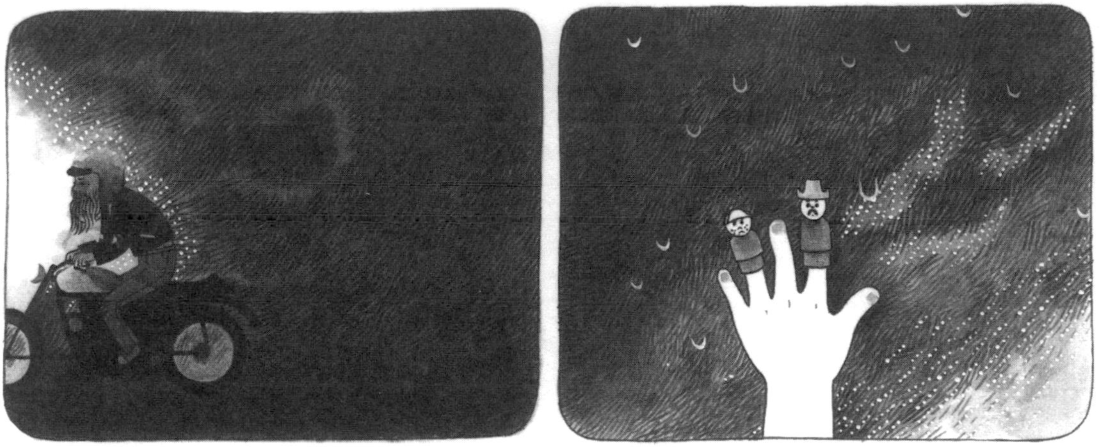

we manage.

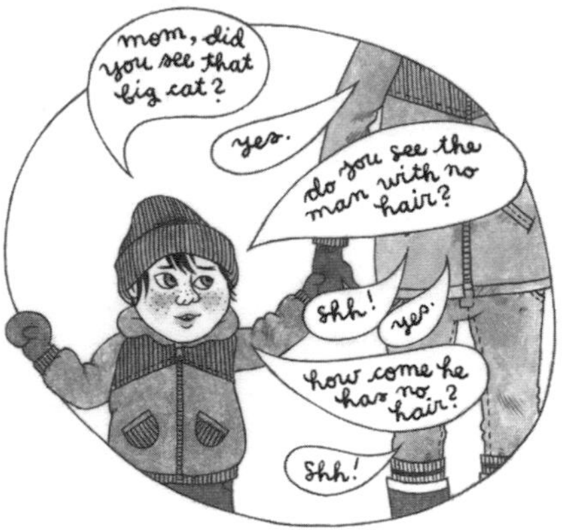
mom, did you see that big cat?
yes.
do you see the man with no hair?
shh!
yes.
how come he has no hair?
shh!

At three or four years old I am already very talkative.

Amère and I mostly get around on foot.

We live near Québec City, right across the river.

When Amère stays up late, she leaves a glass of milk on the kitchen table for me so I can eat my cereal without making a mess.

When there is no milk, I eat my cereal with water.

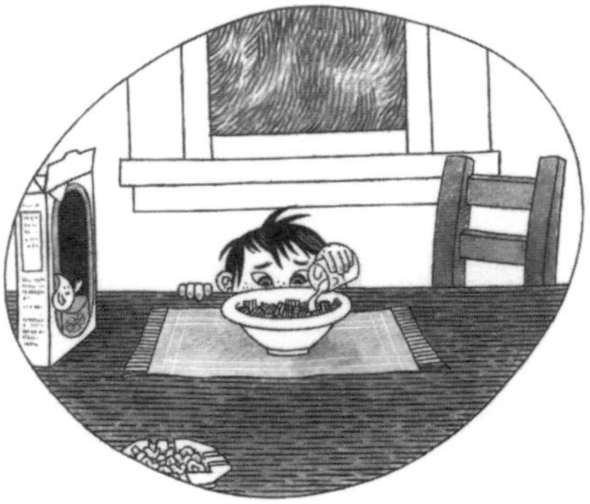

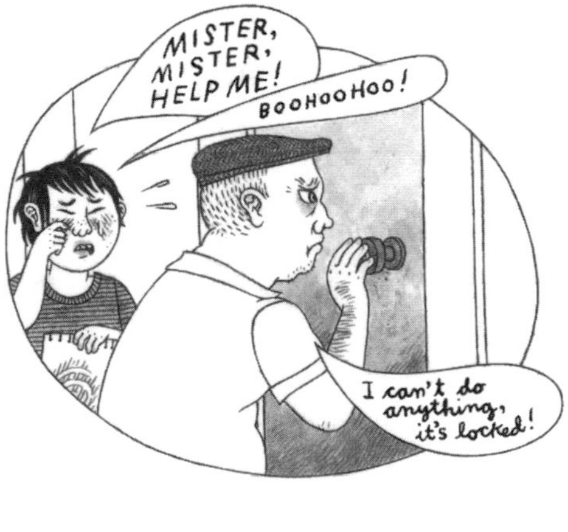
MISTER, MISTER, HELP ME!
BOOHOOHOO!
I can't do anything, it's locked!

I am an early riser.

one morning I go outside for a second and when I come back the door has been locked.

I ask a man on the street to help me.

new year.

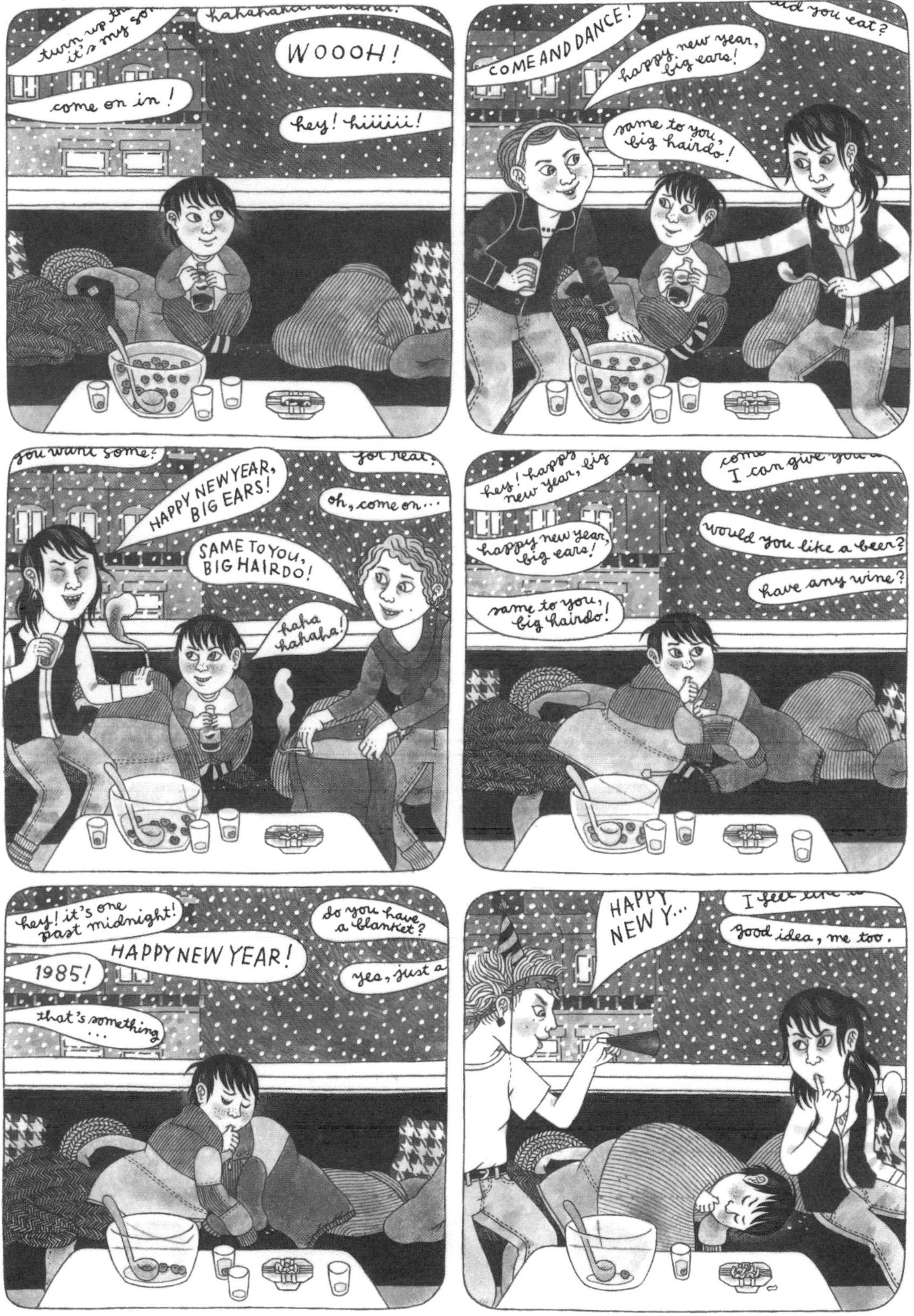
turn up th
it's my so
hahahaha
WOOOH!
come on in!
hey! hiiiiii!
COME AND DANCE!
you eat?
happy new year, big ears!
same to you, big hairdo!
you want some?
for real?
HAPPY NEW YEAR, BIG EARS!
oh, come on...
SAME TO YOU, BIG HAIRDO!
haha hahaha!
hey! happy new year, big
I can give you
happy new year, big ears!
would you like a beer?
have any wine?
same to you, big hairdo!
hey! it's one past midnight!
do you have a blanket?
HAPPY NEW YEAR!
1985!
yes, just a
that's something ...
HAPPY NEW Y...
I feel like
Good idea, me too.

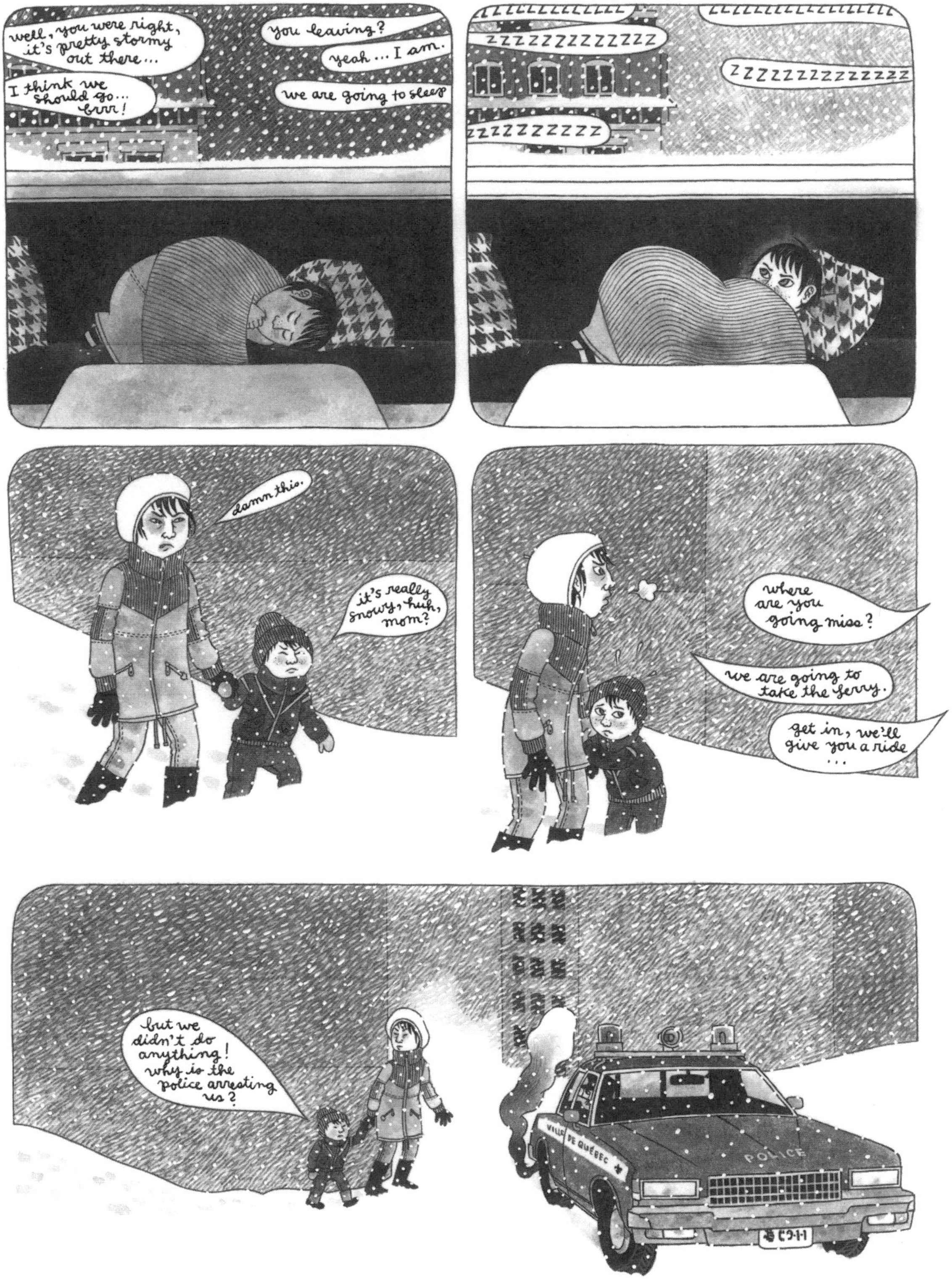

well, you were right, it's pretty stormy out there...
I think we should go... brrr!
You leaving?
yeah... I am.
we are going to sleep
ZZZZZZZZZZZZZZZ
ZZZZZZZZZZZZ
ZZZZZZZZZZZZZZZZZZZZZ
ZZZZZZZZZZZZZZ
ZZZZZZZZZZ
damn this.
it's really snowy, huh, mom?
where are you going miss?
we are going to take the ferry.
get in, we'll give you a ride...
but we didn't do anything! why is the police arresting us?
VILLE DE QUÉBEC
POLICE

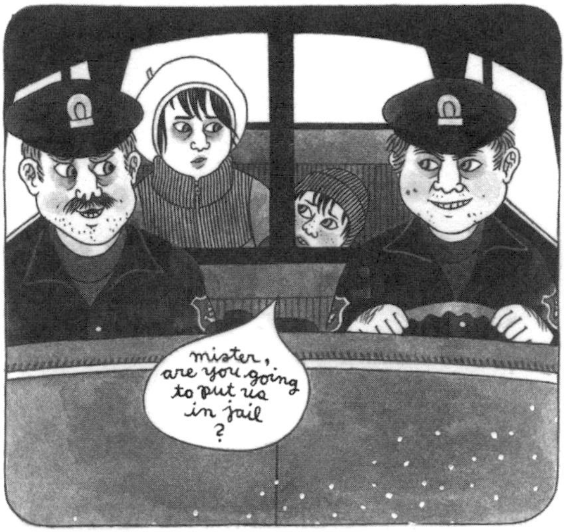
mister, are you going to put us in jail ?

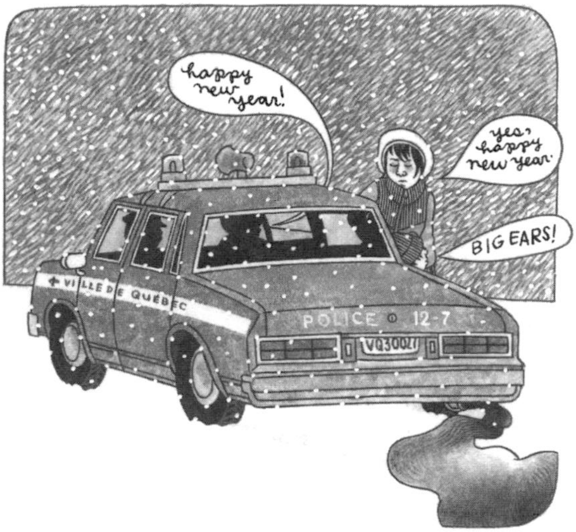
happy new year!
yes, happy new year.
BIG EARS!
VILLE DE QUÉBEC
POLICE 12-7

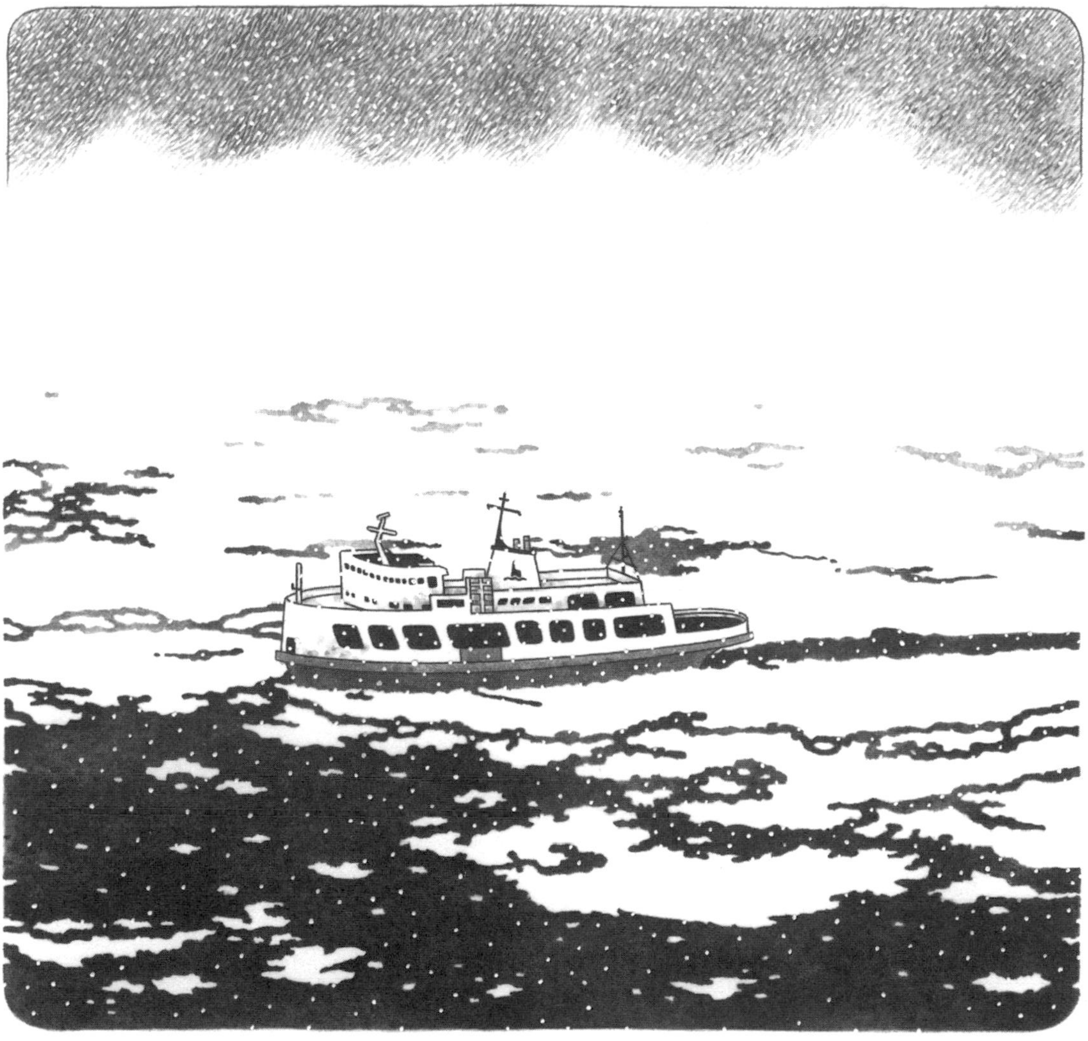

victoria I.

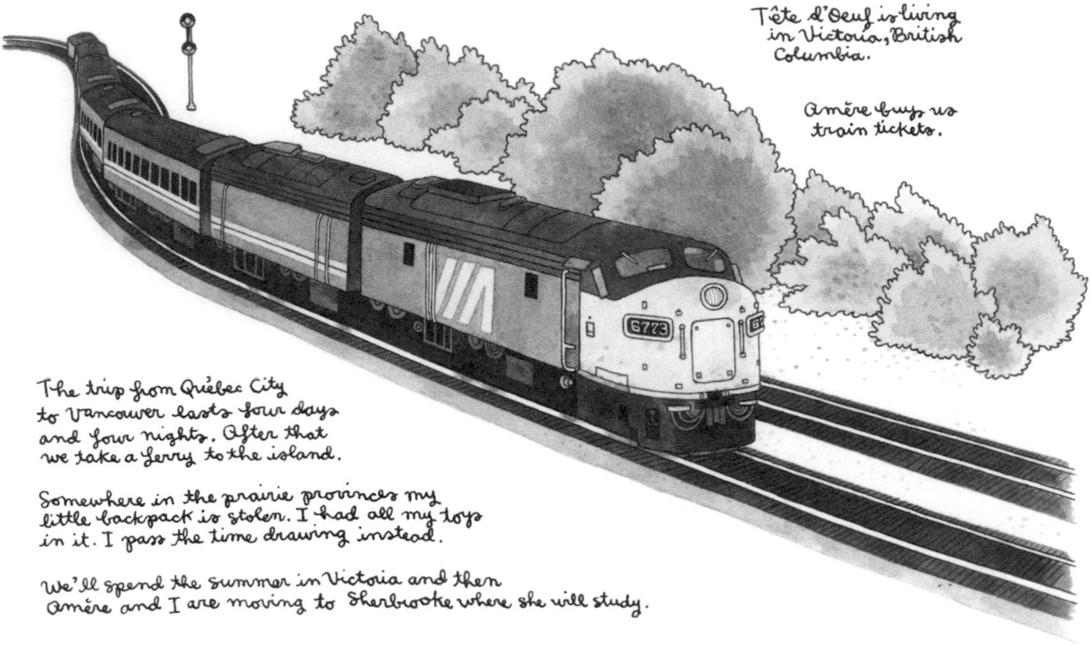

Tête d'Oeuf is living in Victoria, British Columbia.

Amère buys us train tickets.

The trip from Québec City to Vancouver lasts four days and four nights. After that we take a ferry to the island.

Somewhere in the prairie provinces my little backpack is stolen. I had all my toys in it. I pass the time drawing instead.

We'll spend the summer in Victoria and then Amère and I are moving to Sherbrooke where she will study.

My father's house smells like plants. The odor is everywhere, even in my cereal. Tête d'Oeuf doesn't understand my French and I don't understand his English. We mostly communicate through my mother. Sometimes I wake up in the morning when they are just about to go to bed. I watch a lot of TV in English.

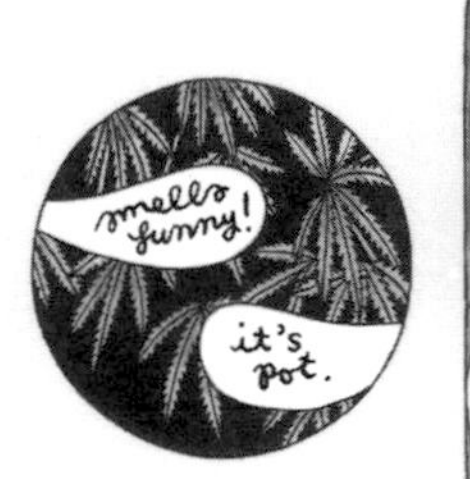
smells funny!
it's pot.

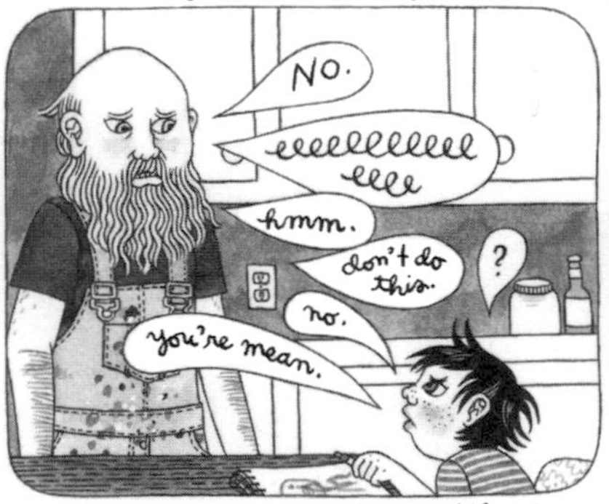
NO.
eeeeeeeeee eee
hmm.
don't do this.
?
no.
you're mean.

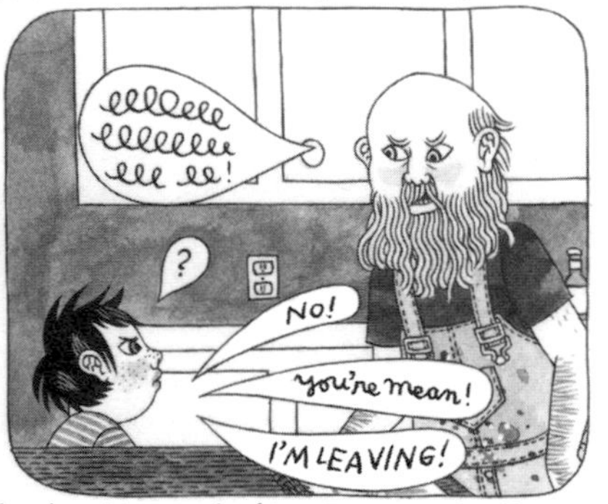
eeeeee eeeeeee eee ee!
?
NO!
you're mean!
I'M LEAVING!

One day I am alone with Tête d'Oeuf and we fight without understanding each other. I go out in the street on my own. I like running away. I have done it often under my mother's watchful eye. At the corner of a busy street I am intercepted by two elderly women, my mother runs behind to catch me.

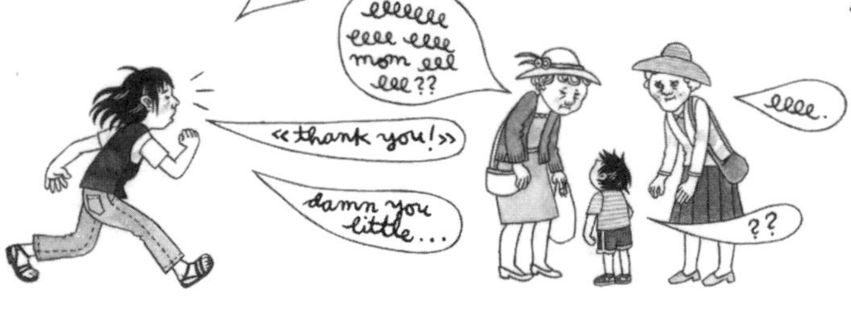
oof!
eeeeee eeee eee mom eee eee??
eeee.
« thank you! »
damn you little...
??

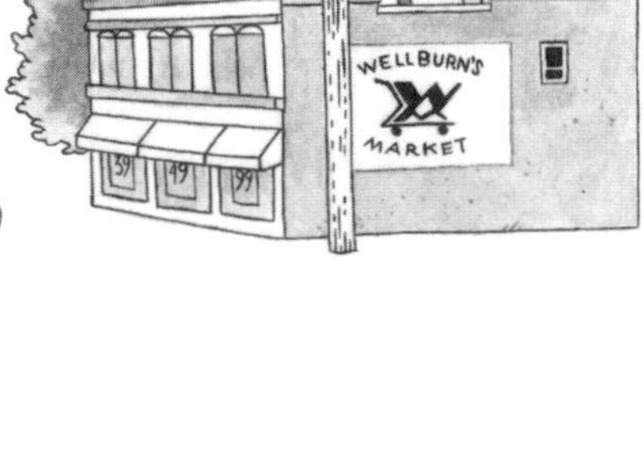
WELLBURN'S MARKET

a nap.

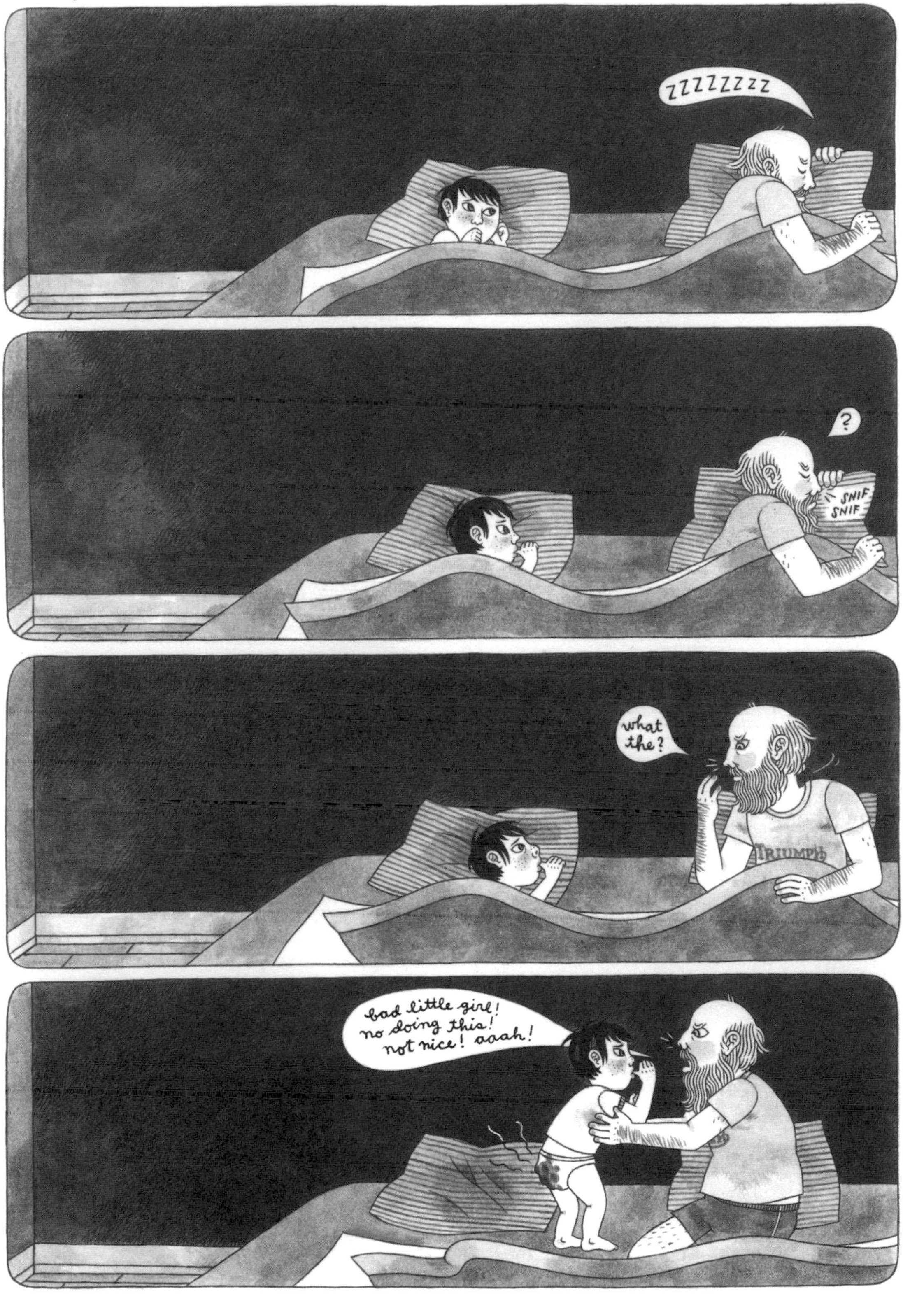
ZZZZZZZZ
?
SNIF SNIF
what the?
TRIUMPH
bad little girl! no doing this! not nice! aaah!

house fire I.

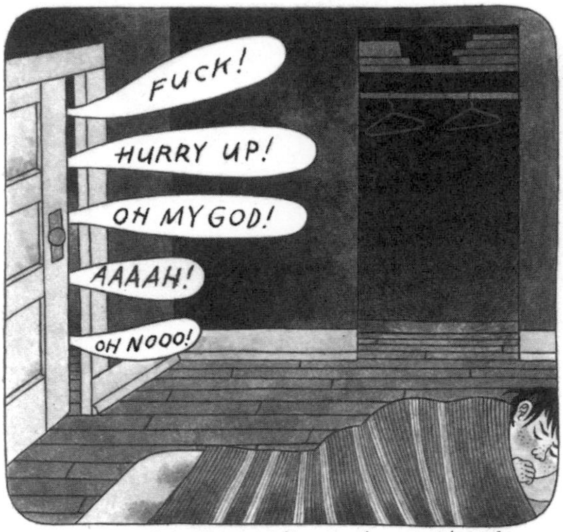
FUCK!
HURRY UP!
OH MY GOD!
AAAAH!
OH NOOO!

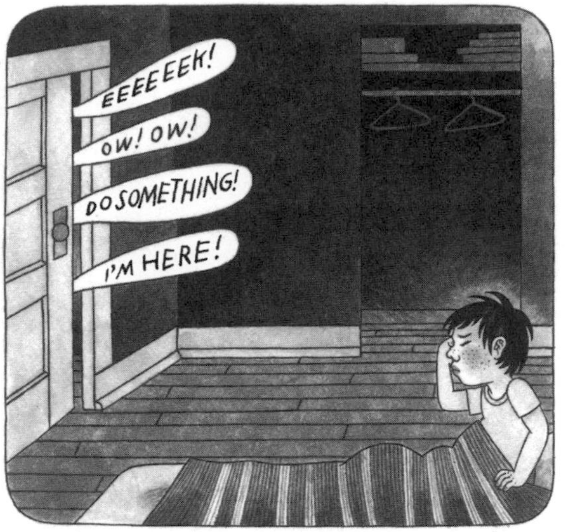
EEEEEEEK!
OW! OW!
DO SOMETHING!
I'M HERE!

I wake up in the middle of the night. It's raining hard, it feels like a lightning storm. I am watching the light play on the hallway wall.

All of a sudden there is a naked man running towards my mother's room with a cooking pot full of water.

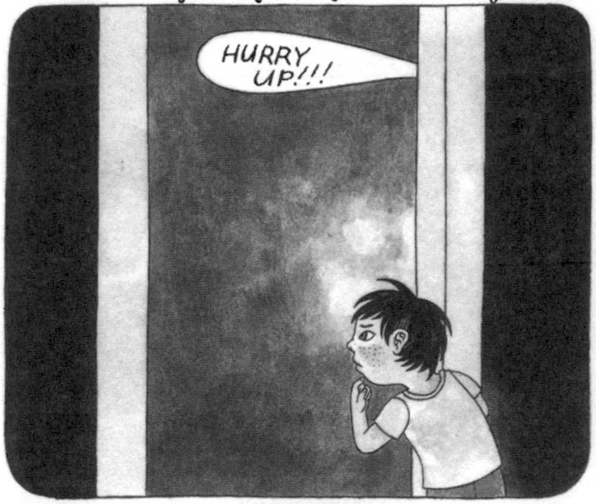
HURRY UP!!!

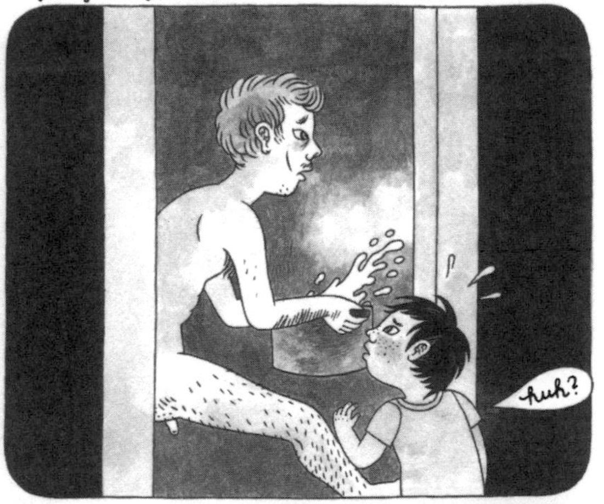
huh?

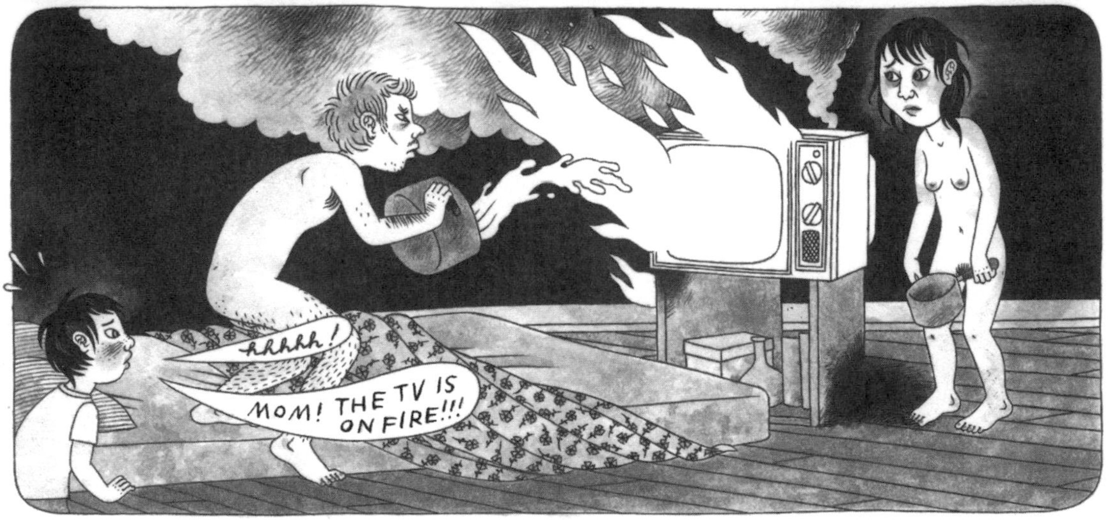
hhhhh!
MOM! THE TV IS ON FIRE!!!

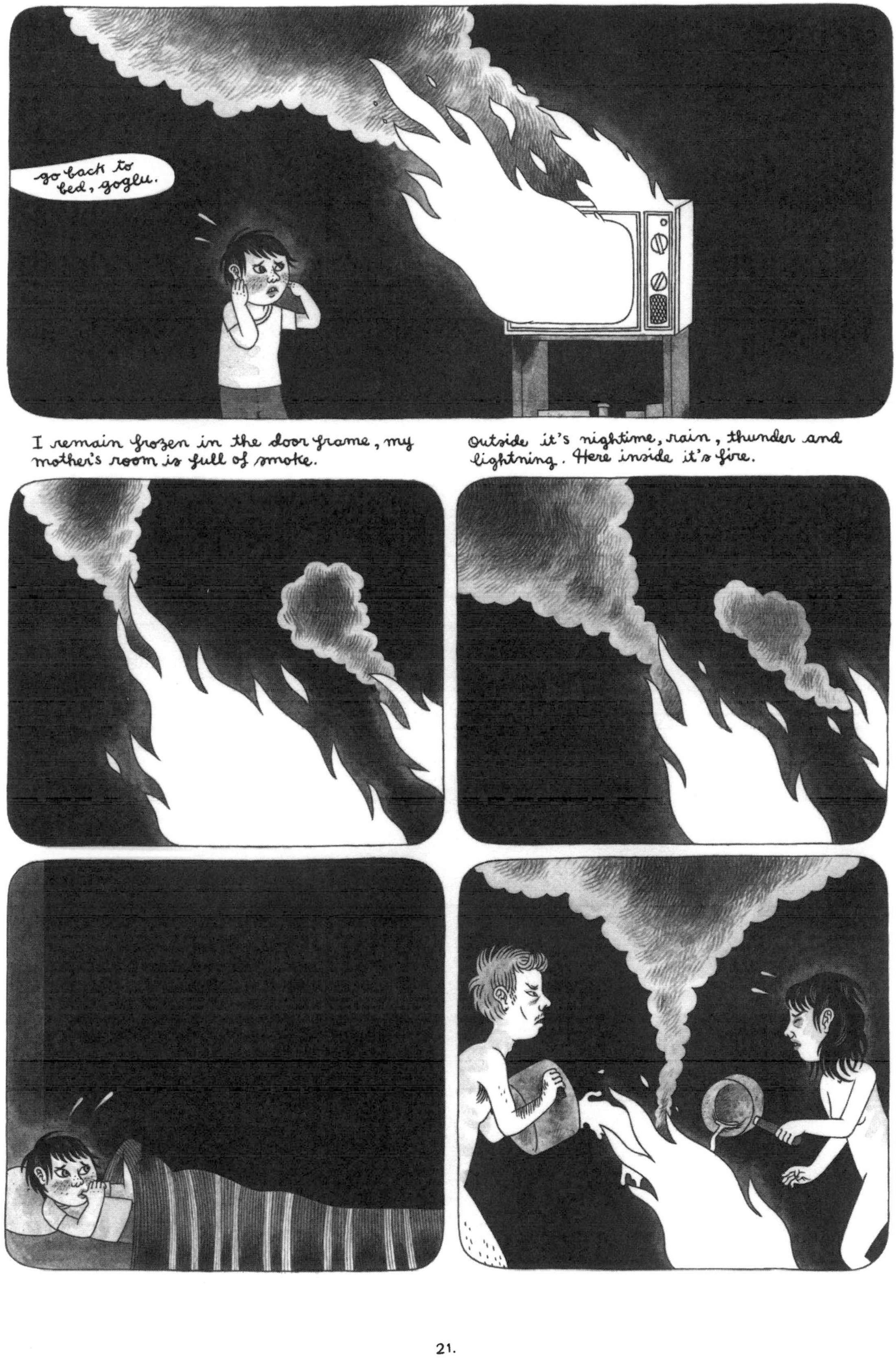
go back to bed, goglu.
I remain frozen in the door frame, my mother's room is full of smoke.
Outside it's nightime, rain, thunder and lightning. Here inside it's fire.

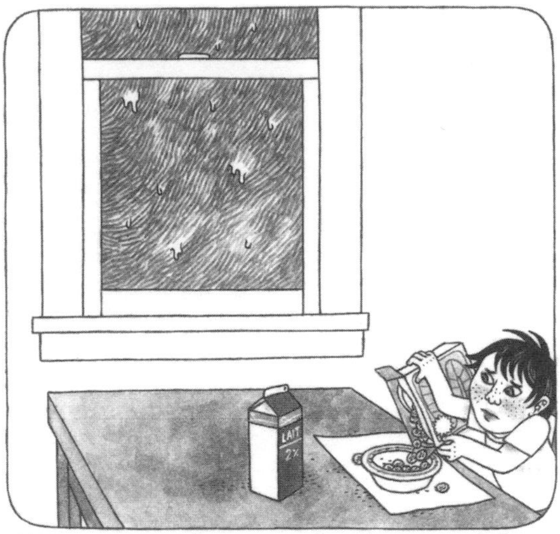

Many surfaces of our apartment are coated with small black particles. My mother tells me that my face is clean.

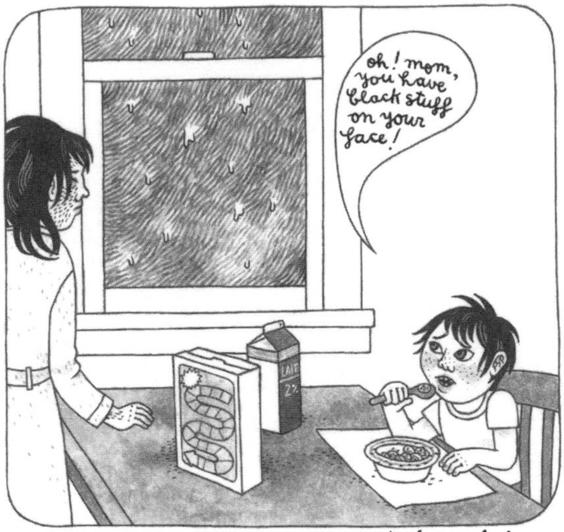
oh! mom, you have black stuff on your face!

Yvan, our landlord, comes over to have a look at the ceiling in our bathroom. It's leaking because of the storm.

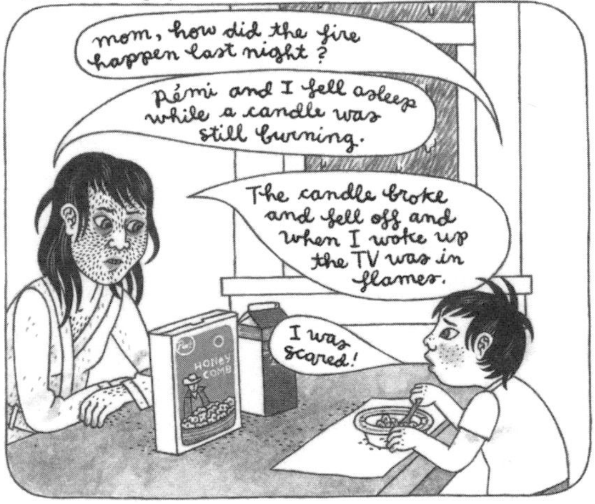
mom, how did the fire happen last night?
Rémi and I fell asleep while a candle was still burning.
The candle broke and fell off and when I woke up the TV was in flames.
I was scared!

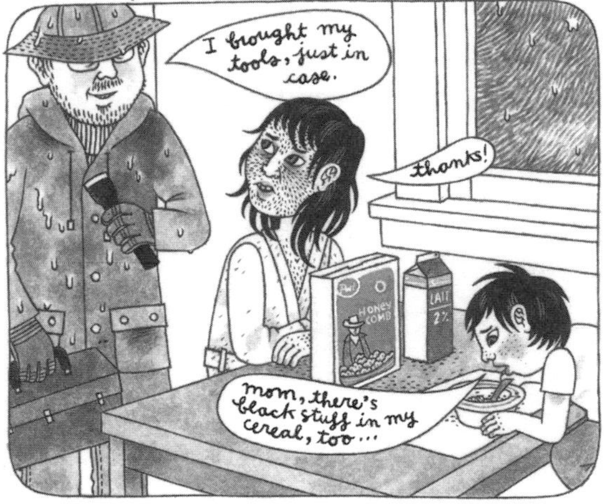
I brought my tools, just in case.
thanks!
mom, there's black stuff in my cereal, too...

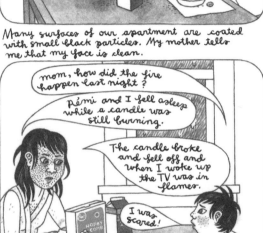

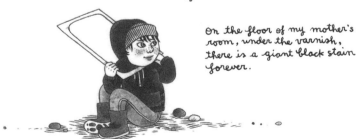

A few days later I play in the alley with what is left of our television.

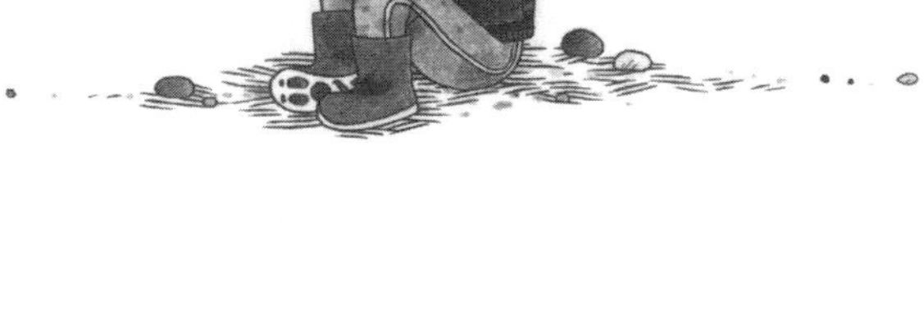

On the floor of my mother's room, under the varnish, there is a giant black stain forever.

goodbye.

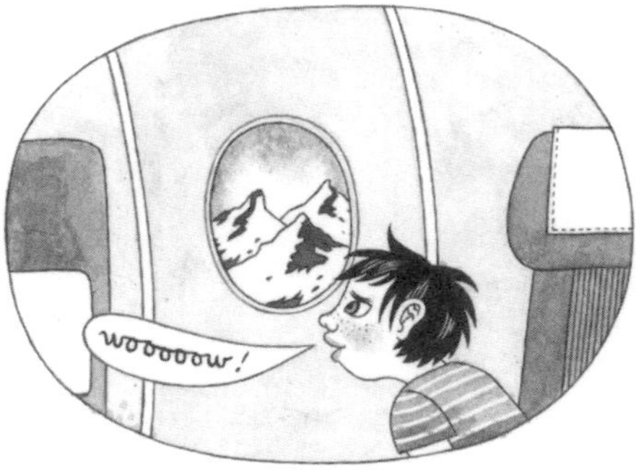
wooooow!

During the summer, Amère and I return to visit Tête d'Oeuf on a plane.

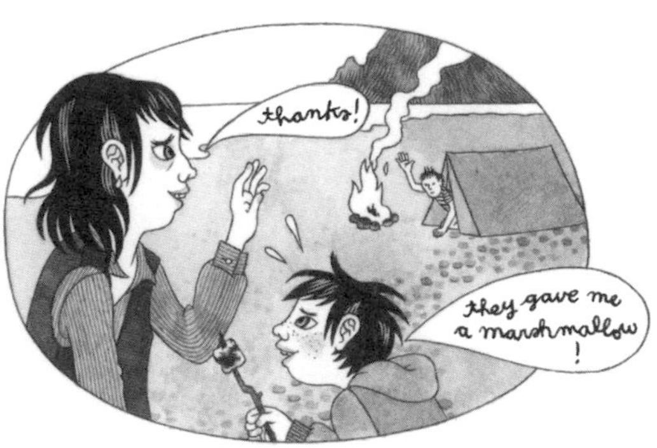
thanks!
they gave me a marshmallow!

The three of us go camping on the Pacific coast. In Tofino we see people from Québec.

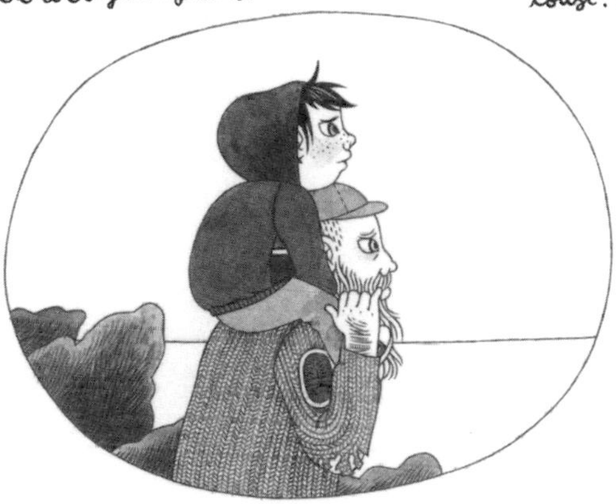

My father is going to see us at Christmas, and then never again.

Tête d'Oeuf is the last person to take me on his shoulders.

At the Vancouver airport we spend the night in the old ambulance my dad drives around.

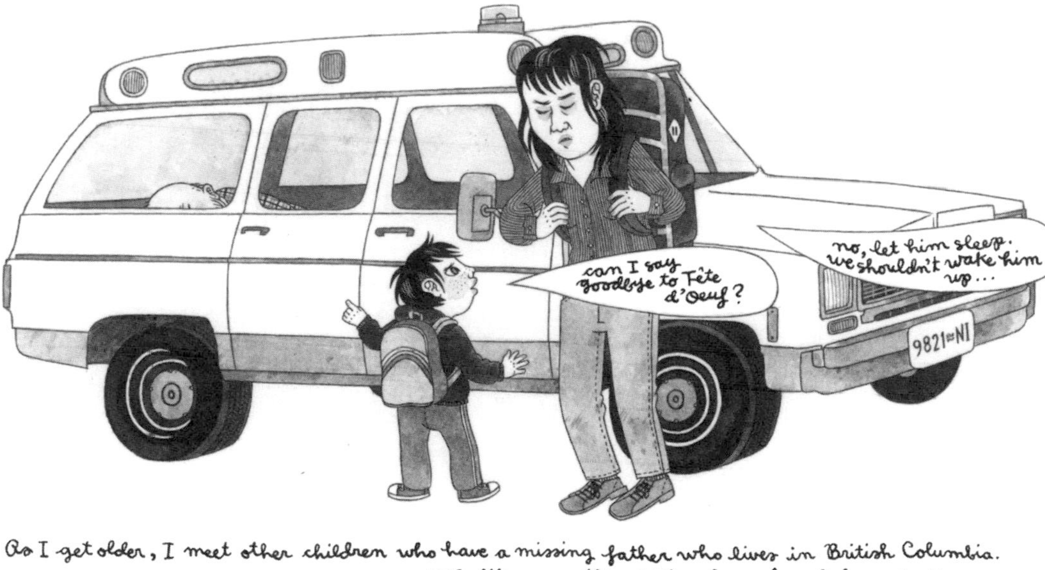
can I say goodbye to Tête d'Oeuf?
no, let him sleep. we shouldn't wake him up...
9821 NI

As I get older, I meet other children who have a missing father who lives in British Columbia. It's like a mythical kingdom where dads go to disappear.

goglu cries.

Amère got a job as a secretary in a factory. I have just started at a special school where I had to pass an entrance exam. I am learning how to read and write and also how to play the violin. Since Amère has to get to work before it is my turn to catch the school bus, she sets our alarm clock every morning so that I know when it is time to leave our house. The front door remains unlocked. We have nothing to steal.

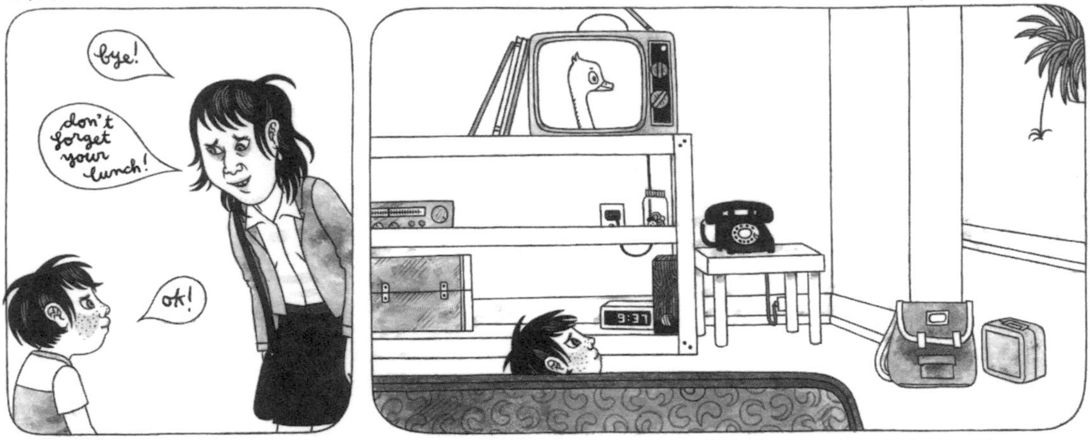

bye!
don't forget your lunch!
ok!
9:37

The routine is the same every day. I watch cartoons until I hear the alarm, I turn it off and I go meet Maude Tardif at our bus stop. She is in the first grade like me. She is mean. She smokes.

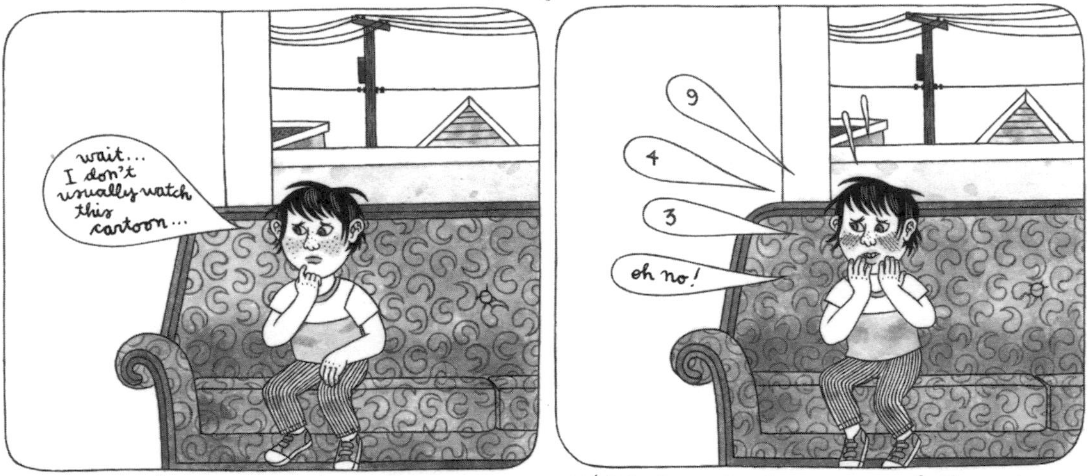

wait... I don't usually watch this cartoon...
9
4
3
oh no!

I am late! what is going on? The alarm didn't go off! School is already scary enough, I am so nervous... I panic, I cry, and then I decide to write Amère a note. I copy some sentences I have learned to read to explain to her that I have gone downstairs to Yvan's, our landlord. He'll know what to do.

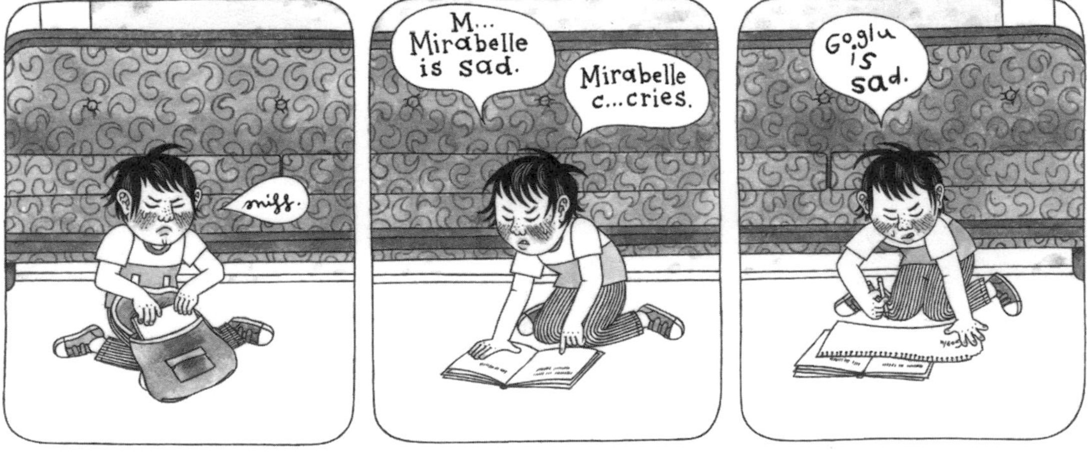

sniff.
M... Mirabelle is sad.
Mirabelle c...cries.
Goglu is sad.

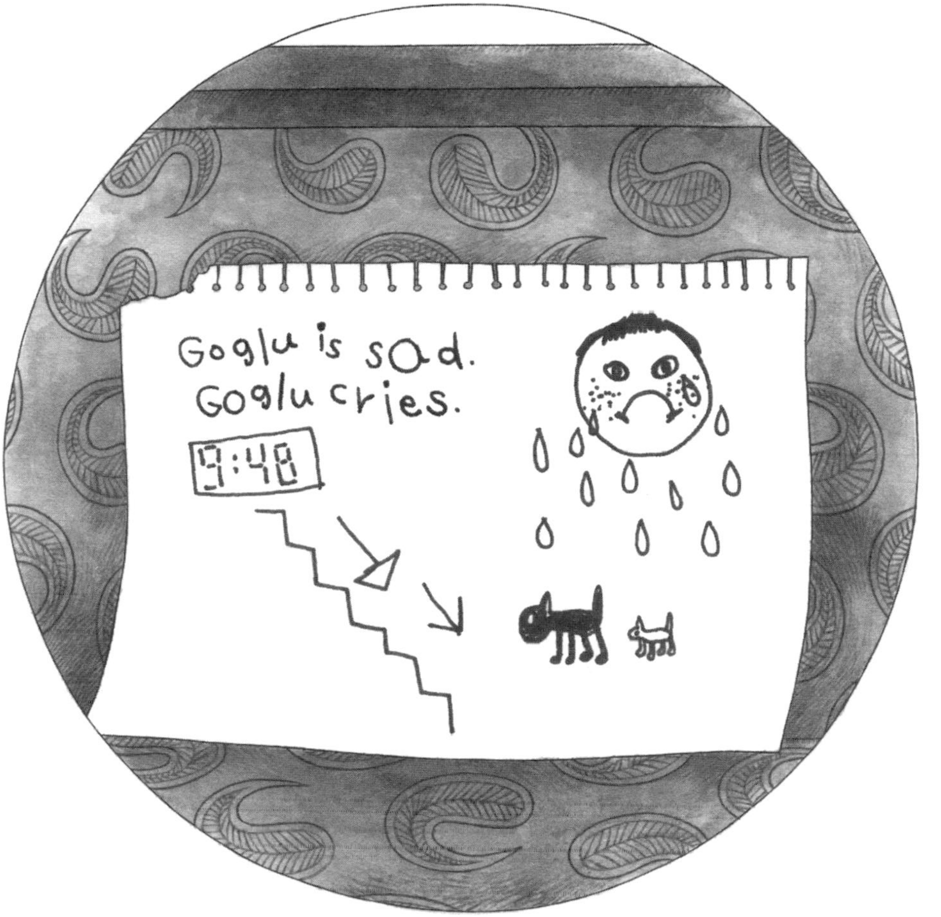
Goglu is sad.
Goglu cries.
9:48

I watch TV all day at the landlord's. At noon I eat my lunch, which I brought with me. My mother comes home in the afternoon, a little earlier than usual. She is very worried, the school called her when they noticed my absence. After a few more late mornings, I am watched by a neighbour.

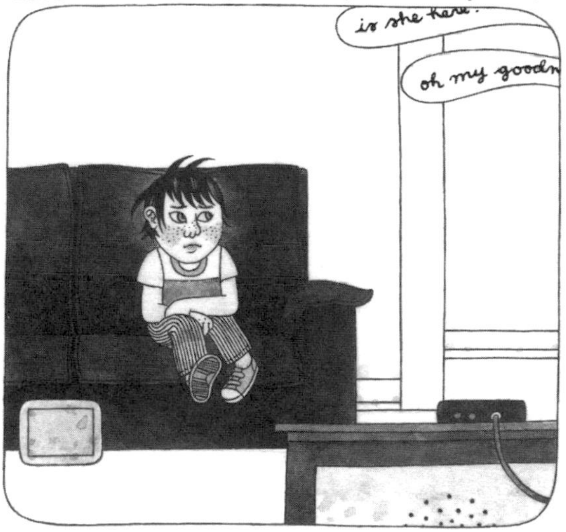
is she here
oh my goodn

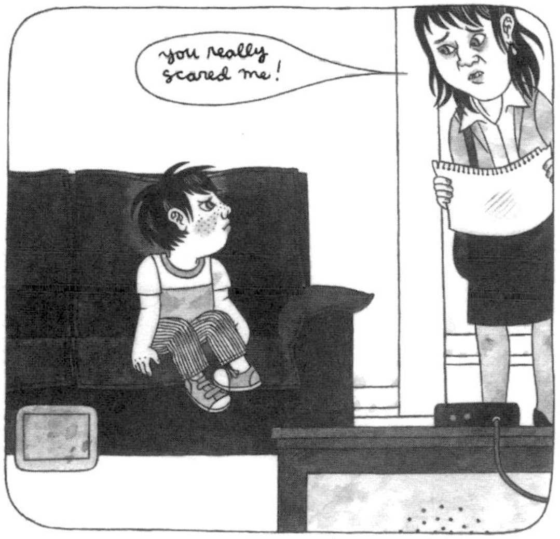
you really scared me!

montréal.

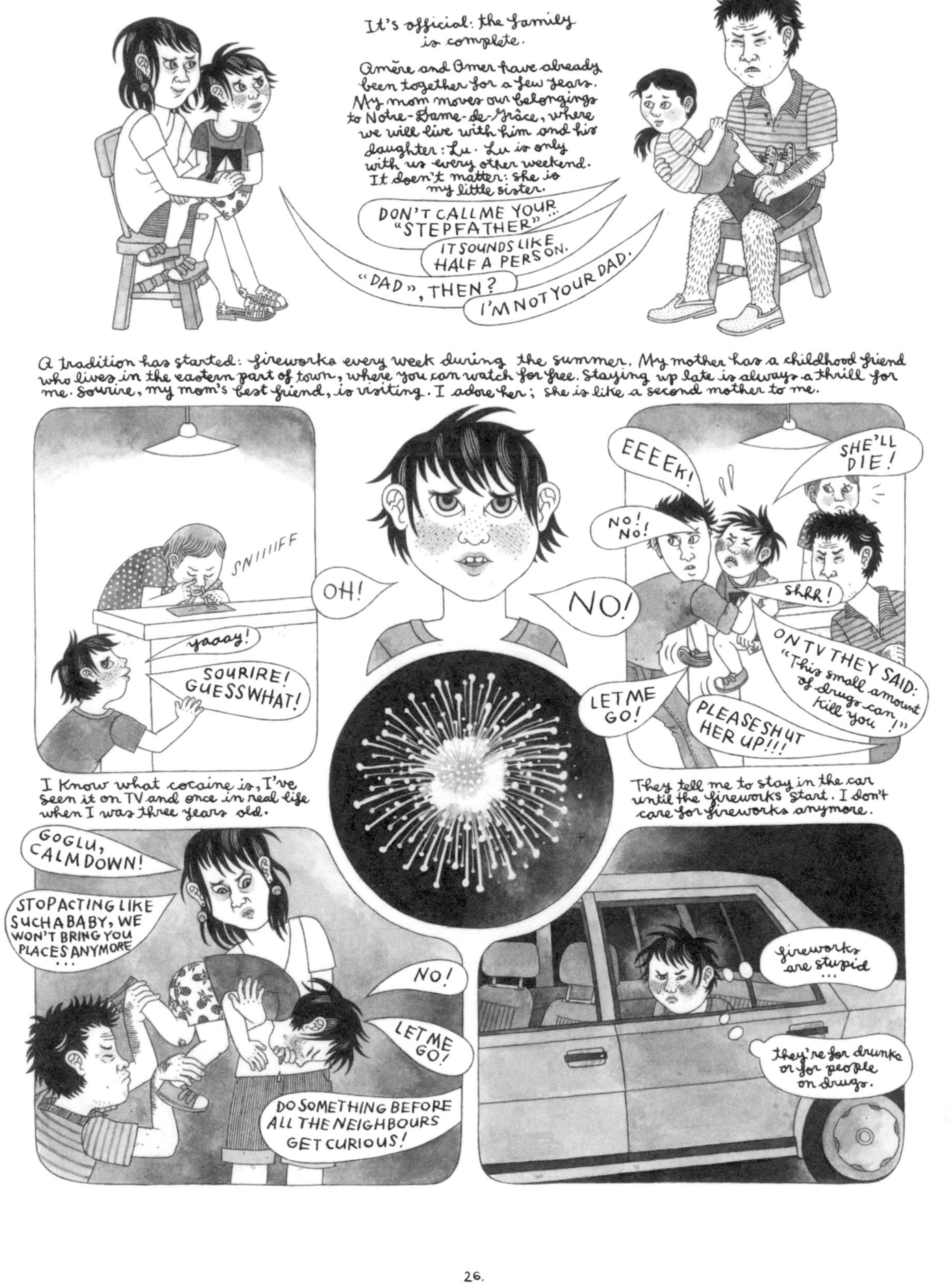
It's official: the family is complete.
Amère and Omer have already been together for a few years. My mom moves our belongings to Notre-Dame-de-Grâce, where we will live with him and his daughter: Lu. Lu is only with us every other weekend. It doesn't matter: she is my little sister.
DON'T CALL ME YOUR "STEPFATHER"...
IT SOUNDS LIKE HALF A PERSON.
«DAD», THEN?
I'M NOT YOUR DAD.
A tradition has started: fireworks every week during the summer. My mother has a childhood friend who lives in the eastern part of town, where you can watch for free. Staying up late is always a thrill for me. Sourire, my mom's best friend, is visiting. I adore her; she is like a second mother to me.
SNIIIIFF
yaaay!
SOURIRE! GUESS WHAT!
OH!
NO!
EEEEK!
NO! NO!
SHE'LL DIE!
SHRR!
ON TV THEY SAID: "This small amount of drugs can kill you!"
LET ME GO!
PLEASE SHUT HER UP!!!
I know what cocaine is, I've seen it on TV and once in real life when I was three years old.
They tell me to stay in the car until the fireworks start. I don't care for fireworks anymore.
GOGLU, CALM DOWN!
STOP ACTING LIKE SUCH A BABY, WE WON'T BRING YOU PLACES ANYMORE...
NO!
LET ME GO!
DO SOMETHING BEFORE ALL THE NEIGHBOURS GET CURIOUS!
fireworks are stupid...
they're for drunks or for people on drugs.

polytechnique.

On the news they are telling us about a madman who has gone into an engineering school here in Montréal to shoot women, killing fourteen of them. The city, the province, the country are in shock. Everyone is mourning. In his suicide note the shooter claims that "feminists have ruined his life".

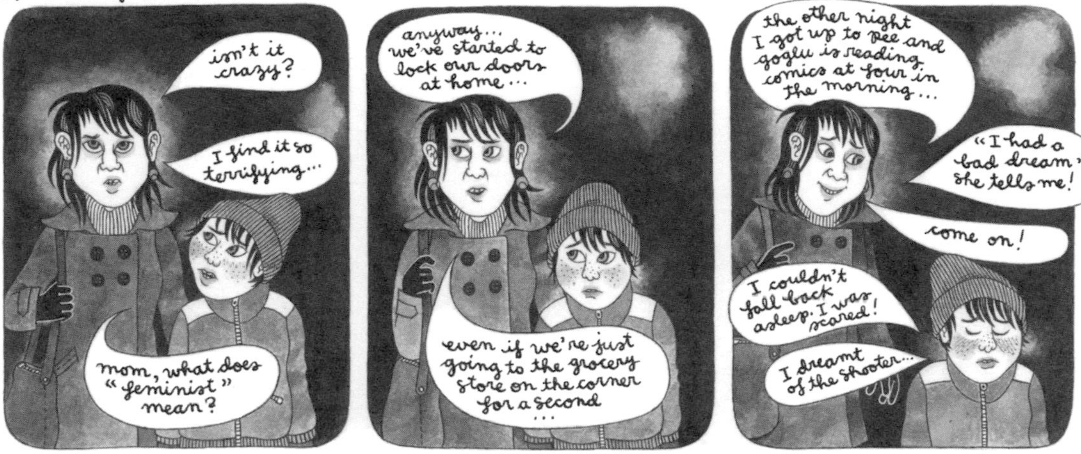

isn't it crazy?
I find it so terrifying...
mom, what does "feminist" mean?
anyway... we've started to lock our doors at home...
even if we're just going to the grocery store on the corner for a second ...
the other night I got up to pee and goglu is reading comics at four in the morning...
"I had a bad dream" she tells me!
come on!
I couldn't fall back asleep. I was scared!
I dreamt of the shooter...

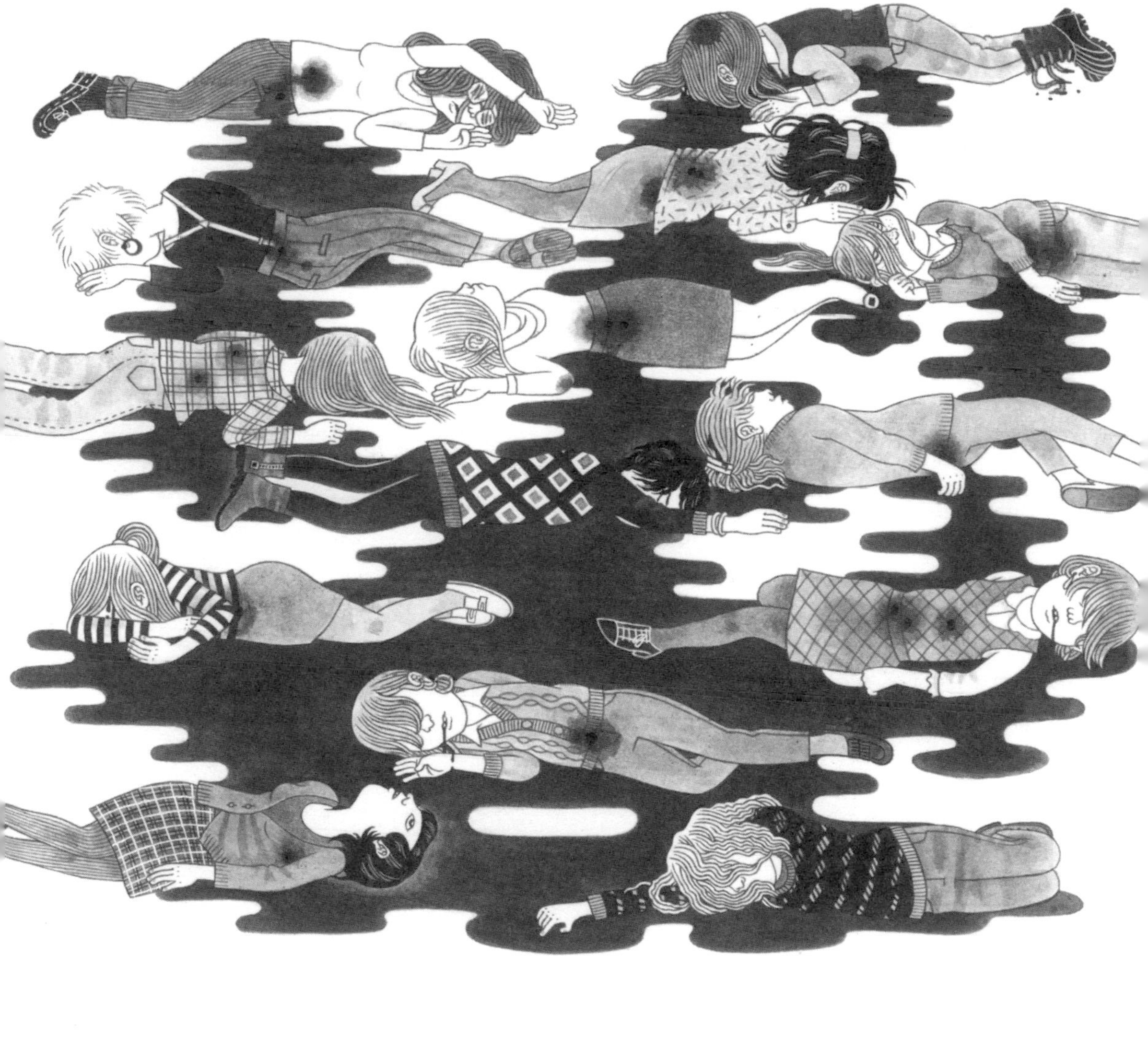

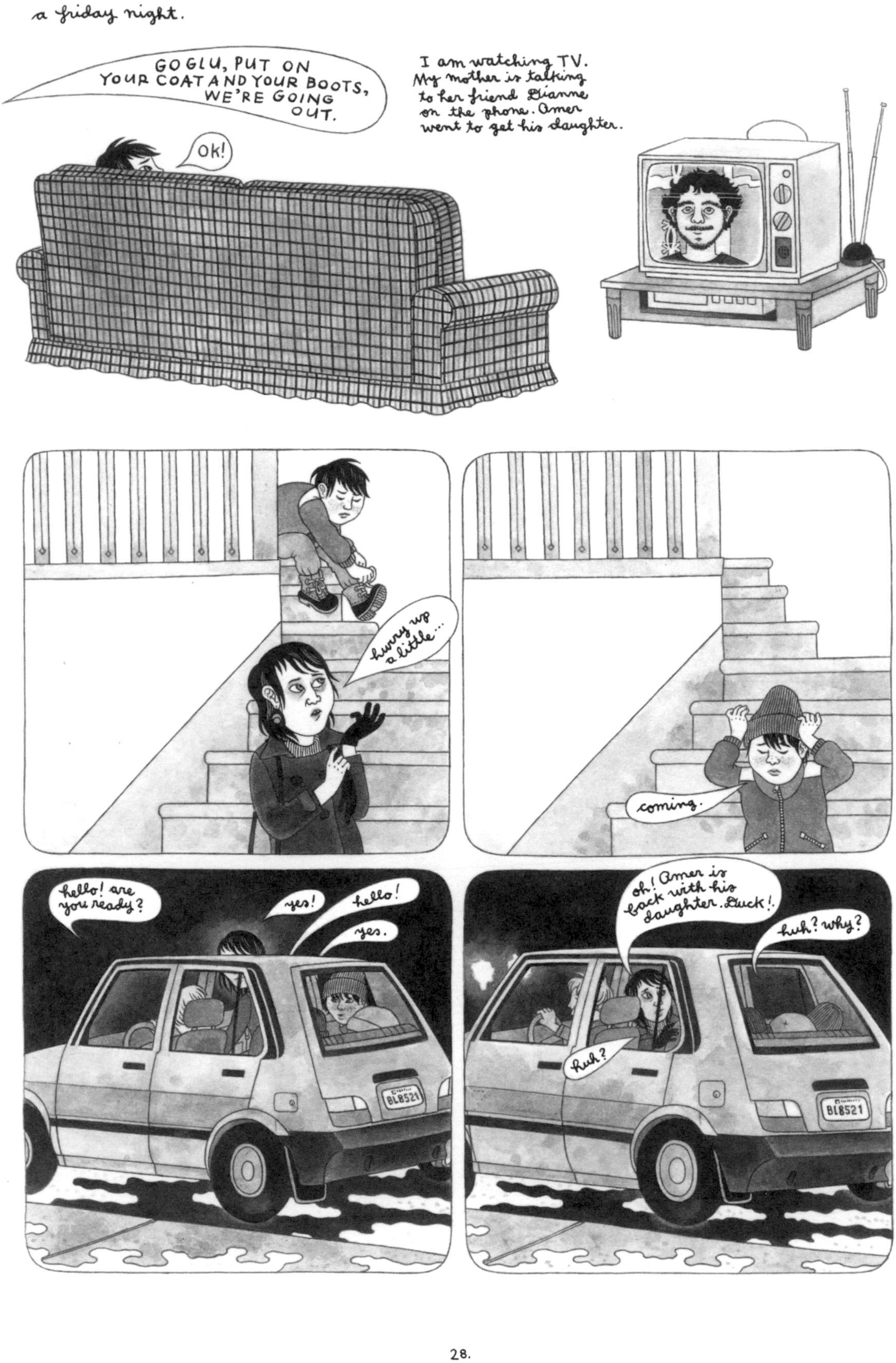
a friday night.
GOGLU, PUT ON YOUR COAT AND YOUR BOOTS, WE'RE GOING OUT.
OK!
I am watching TV. My mother is talking to her friend Dianne on the phone. Amer went to get his daughter.
hurry up a little...
coming.
hello! are you ready?
yes!
hello!
yes.
oh! Amer is back with his daughter. Duck!
huh? why?
huh?
BL8521

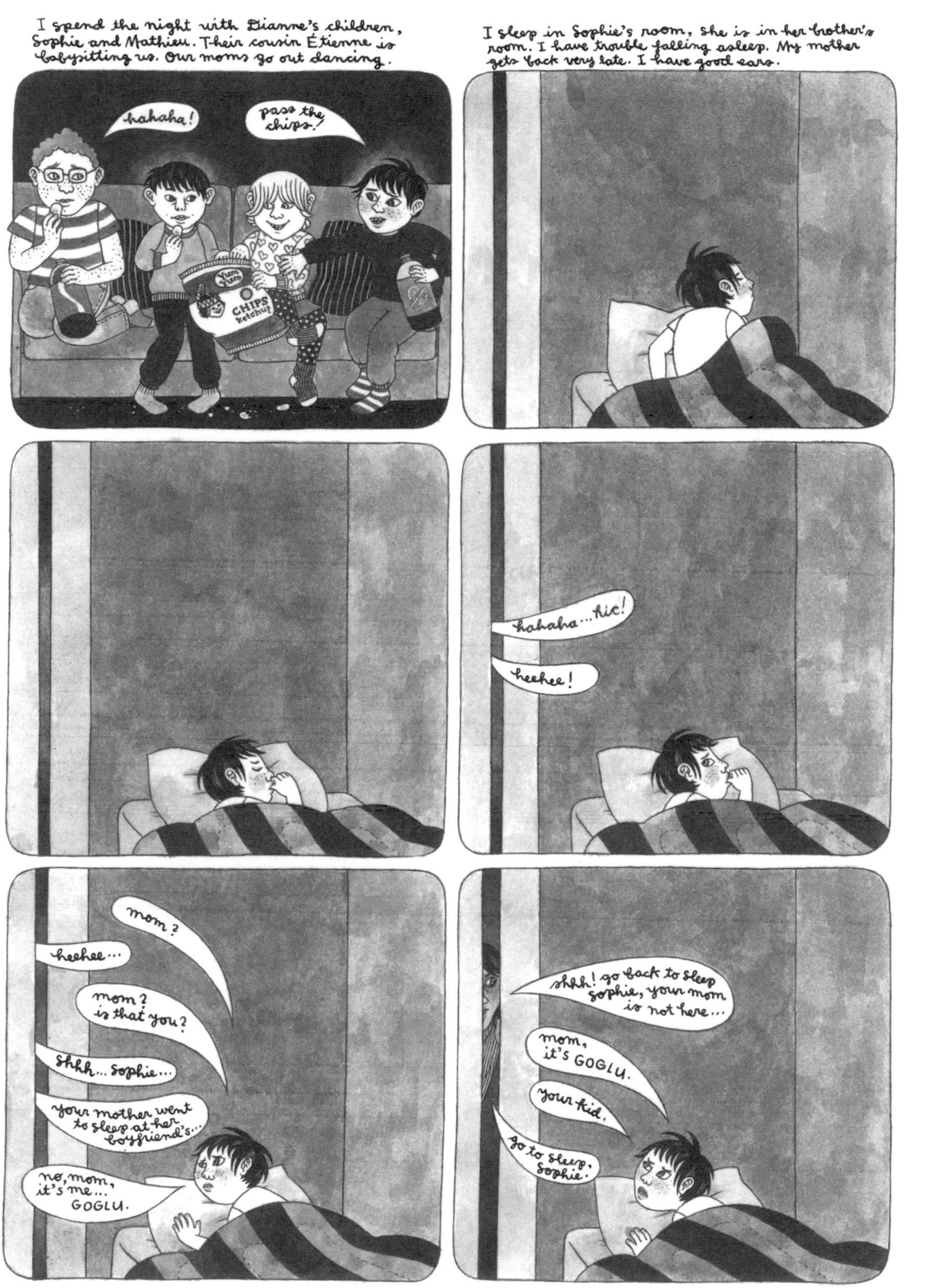
I spend the night with Dianne's children, Sophie and Mathieu. Their cousin Étienne is babysitting us. Our moms go out dancing.
hahaha!
pass the chips!
CHIPS ketchup
I sleep in Sophie's room, she is in her brother's room. I have trouble falling asleep. My mother gets back very late. I have good ears.
hahaha... hic!
heehee!
mom?
heehee...
mom? is that you?
shhh... sophie...
your mother went to sleep at her boyfriend's...
no, mom, it's me... GOGLU.
shhh! go back to sleep sophie, your mom is not here...
mom, it's GOGLU.
your kid.
go to sleep, sophie.

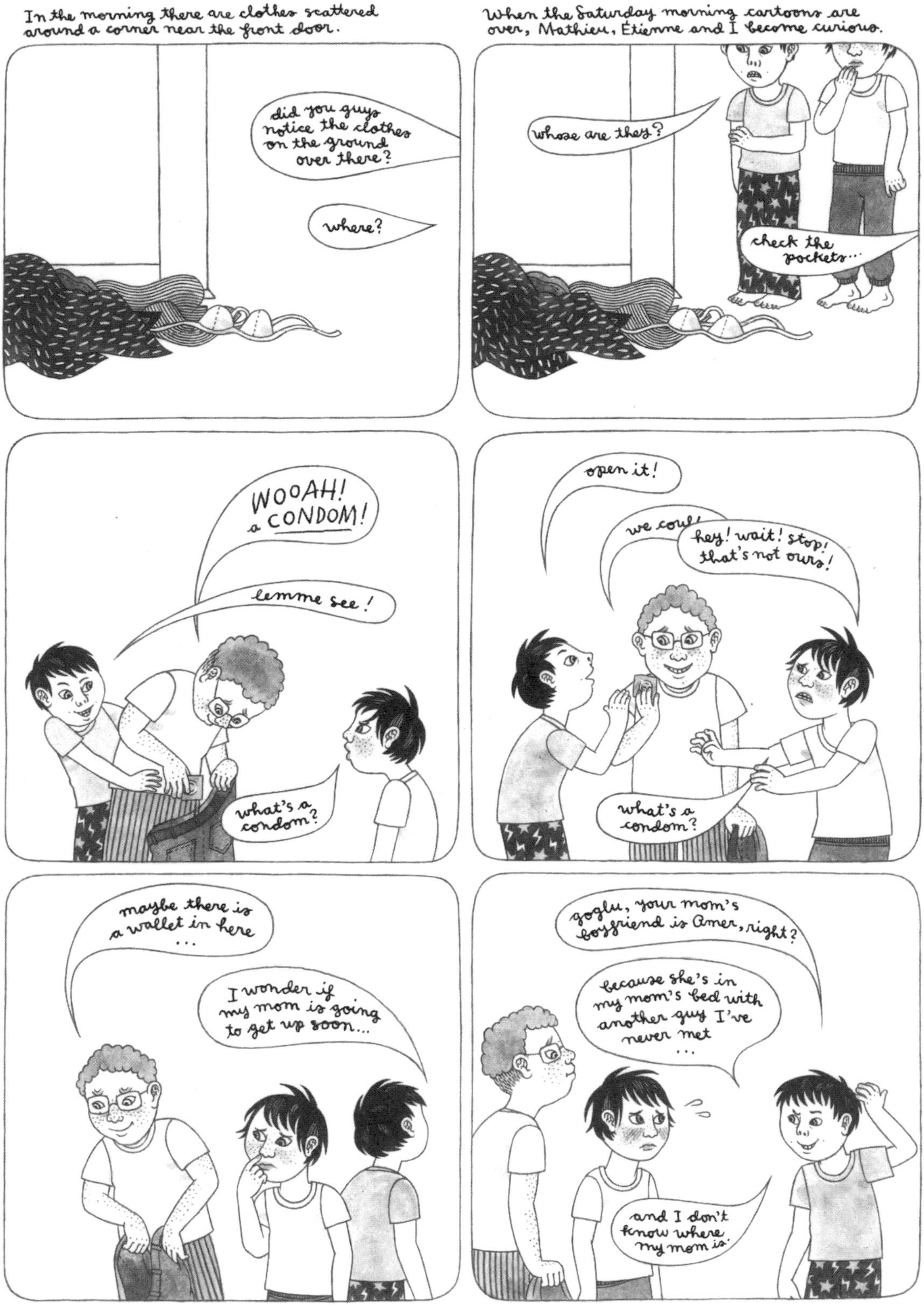
In the morning there are clothes scattered around a corner near the front door.
did you guys notice the clothes on the ground over there?
where?
When the Saturday morning cartoons are over, Mathieu, Étienne and I become curious.
Whose are they?
check the pockets...
WOOAH! a CONDOM!
lemme see!
what's a condom?
open it!
we coul
hey! wait! stop! that's not ours!
what's a condom?
maybe there is a wallet in here ...
I wonder if my mom is going to get up soon...
goglu, your mom's boyfriend is Amer, right?
because she's in my mom's bed with another guy I've never met ...
and I don't know where my mom is.

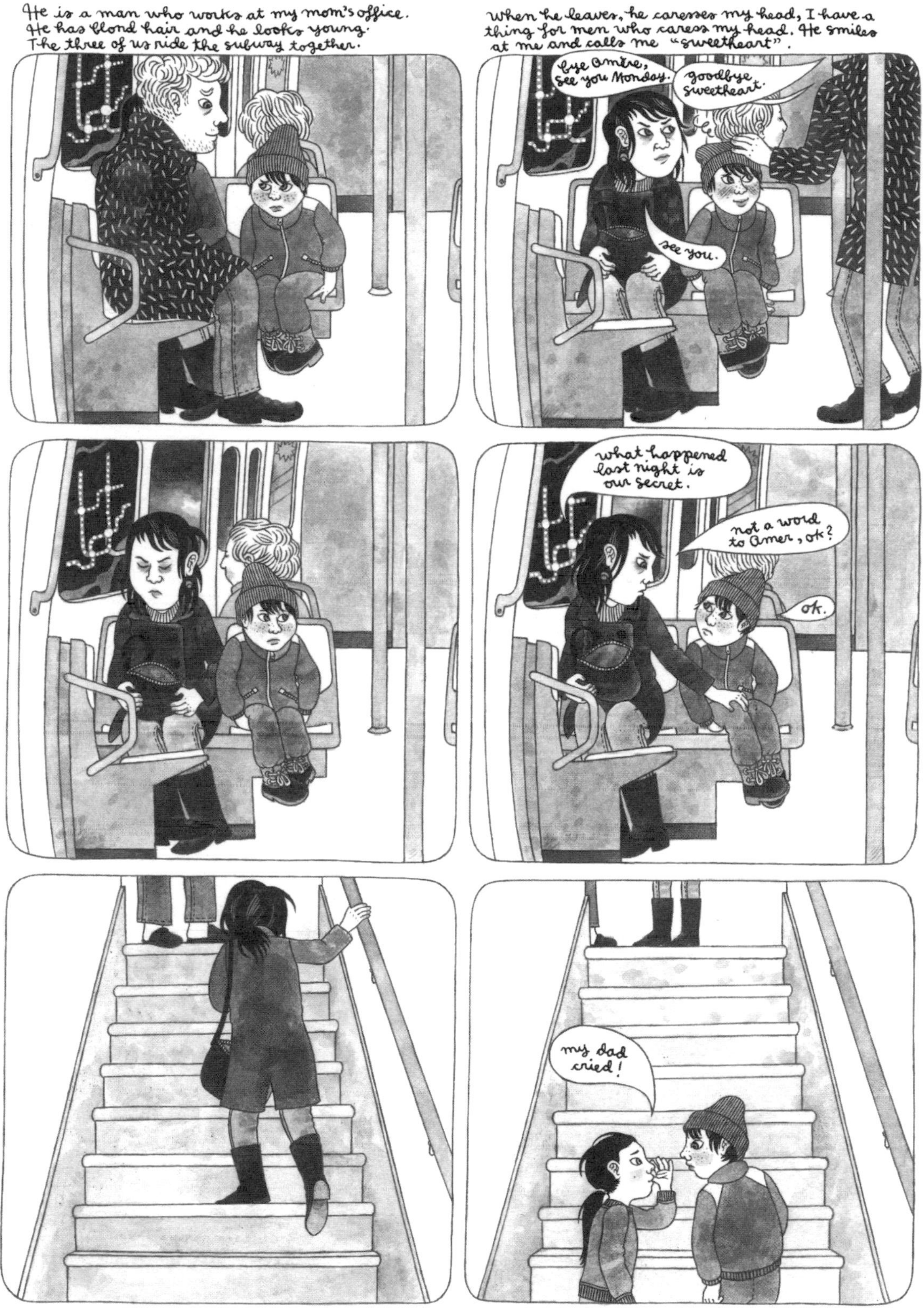
He is a man who works at my mom's office. He has blond hair and he looks young. The three of us ride the subway together.
When he leaves, he caresses my head, I have a thing for men who caress my head. He smiles at me and calls me "sweetheart".
bye Amère, see you Monday.
goodbye sweetheart.
see you.
what happened last night is our secret.
not a word to Amer, ok?
ok.
my dad cried!

Once we are back at home,
àmère goes to bed.

house fire II.

It's St. John the Baptist Day, Québec's national holiday.

At my house it is a big deal, I come from a family of separatists.

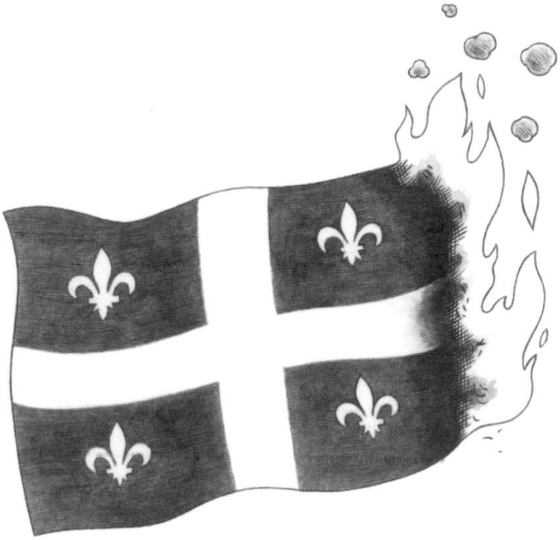

Now that anarchy has been explained to me, I see myself as an anarchist.

My friend's house is burning across the street.

Rumours are circulating around the neighbourhood that someone has set fire to the fleurdelisé* that was hanging from the balcony on the second floor. The owners deny it. Someone told me that in cases of arson the insurance company does not pay. Luckily for her, my friend is traveling abroad...

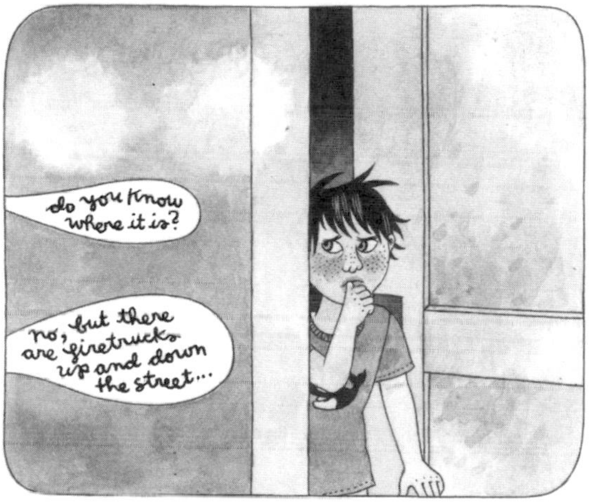

do you know where it is?
no, but there are firetrucks up and down the street...

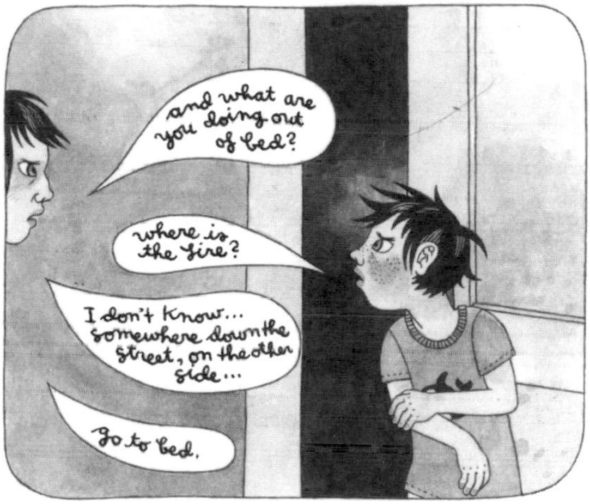

and what are you doing out of bed?
where is the fire?
I don't know... somewhere down the street, on the other side...
Go to bed.

Amer and Amère have bought a house in a suburb on the South Shore where all is quieter. Amer says that more and more immigrants are moving near where we live. It bothers him. Our new house has an above-ground pool and a garden. Everyone tells me how lucky I am.

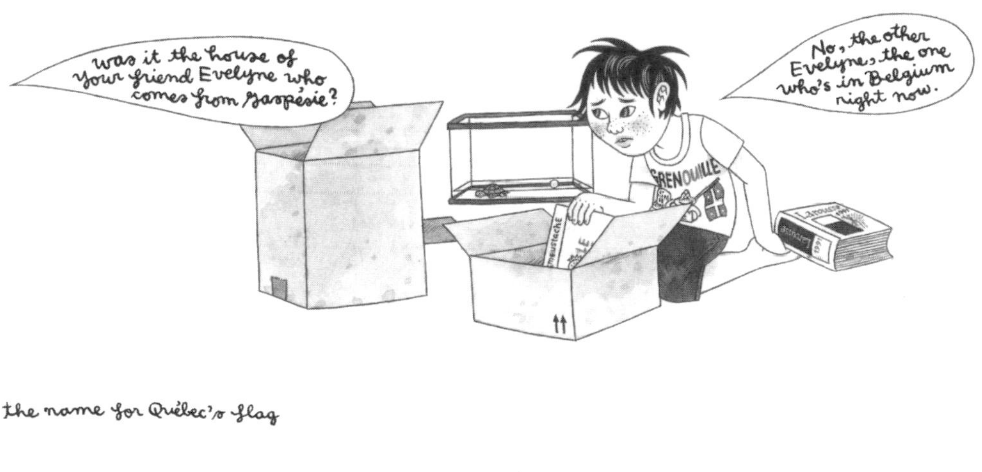

Was it the house of your friend Evelyne who comes from Gaspésie?
No, the other Evelyne, the one who's in Belgium right now.
GRENOUILLE

* the name for Québec's flag

in the suburbs
my mother signs me
up for day camp
for the summer.

I love it.

we have activities in
the woods and park
near my house.

I mostly get along
with my camp counselors,
young men and women.

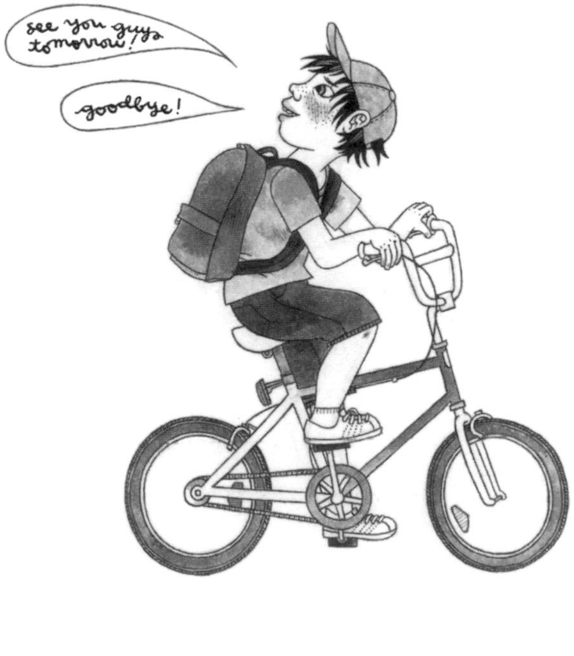
see you guys tomorrow!
goodbye!

I hear.

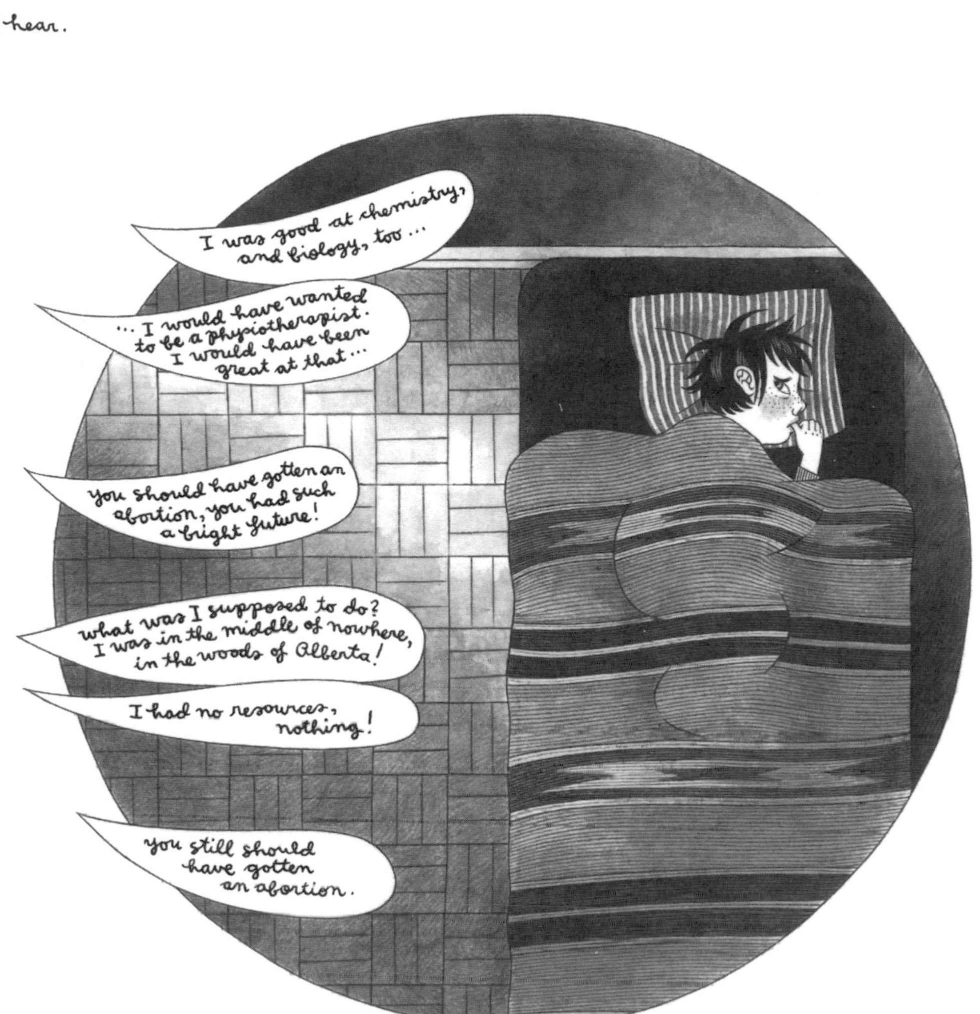
I was good at chemistry, and biology, too...
... I would have wanted to be a physiotherapist. I would have been great at that...
you should have gotten an abortion, you had such a bright future!
what was I supposed to do? I was in the middle of nowhere, in the woods of Alberta!
I had no resources, nothing!
you still should have gotten an abortion.

Amère has her driver's license now so sometimes on week nights we go to the public library. These moments spent alone together are precious. I call her at work every day after school, it's our time to talk to each other because by the time she gets home she is often too tired.

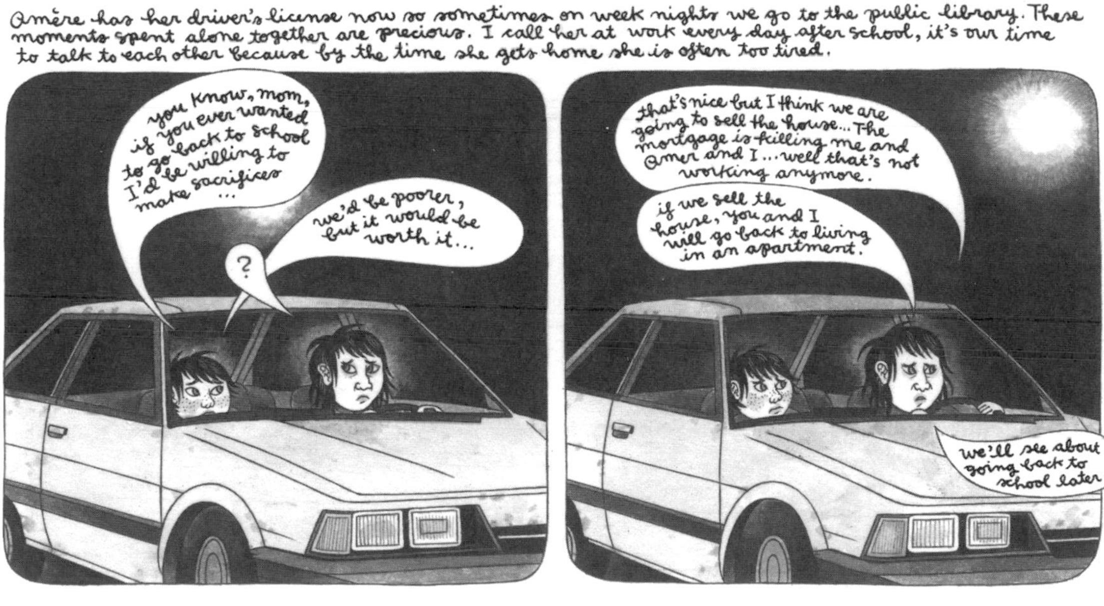
you know, mom, if you ever wanted to go back to school I'd be willing to make sacrifices...
?
we'd be poorer, but it would be worth it...
that's nice but I think we are going to sell the house... The mortgage is killing me and Amer and I... well that's not working anymore.
if we sell the house, you and I will go back to living in an apartment.
we'll see about going back to school later.

mummy.

I am watching a movie on TV in the basement. Amer, his brother, and my mother are in the kitchen. They are drinking red wine and smoking hash. I pretend not to know what they are doing. I don't like it. At school and on TV we are warned incessantly: people who take drugs can end up in jail.

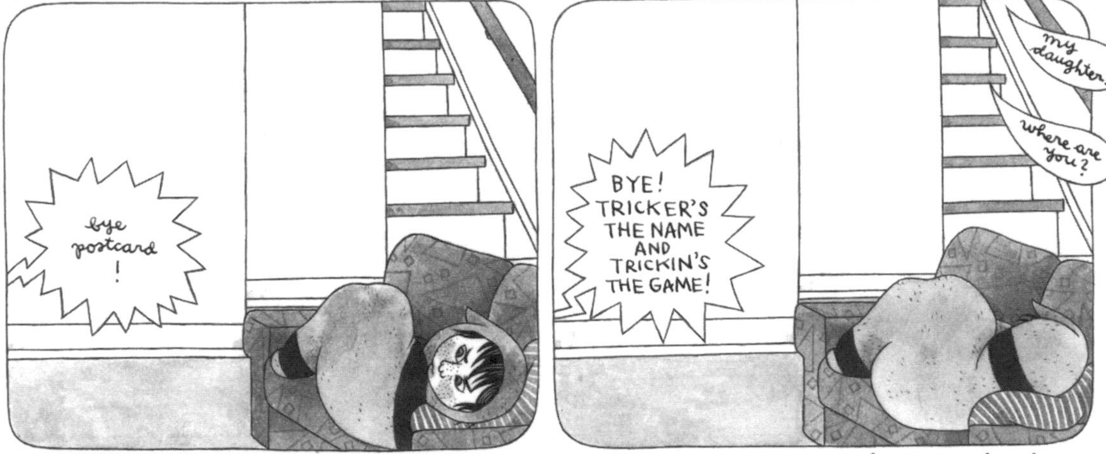
bye postcard !
BYE! TRICKER'S THE NAME AND TRICKIN'S THE GAME!
my daughter!
where are you?

Amère only does this kind of stuff on weekends, to relax. I still wish I was somewhere else. When she drinks, she often needs a friend, so she comes and finds me, wanting us to play together. I hide my nose. The wine and hash on her breath smell a little bit like she ate a turd...

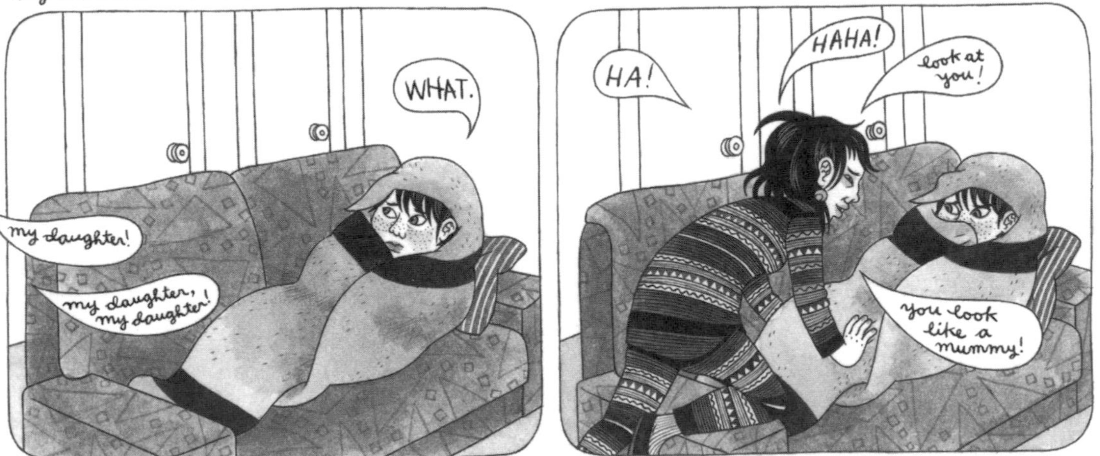
my daughter!
my daughter, my daughter!
WHAT.
HA!
HAHA!
look at you!
you look like a mummy!

I don't know how to go about watching my movie quietly. Whatever I say, it will make her sad, or worse, angry. She wants to wrestle with me and it gives me the idea to take her on my back to the kitchen, where the other adults are.

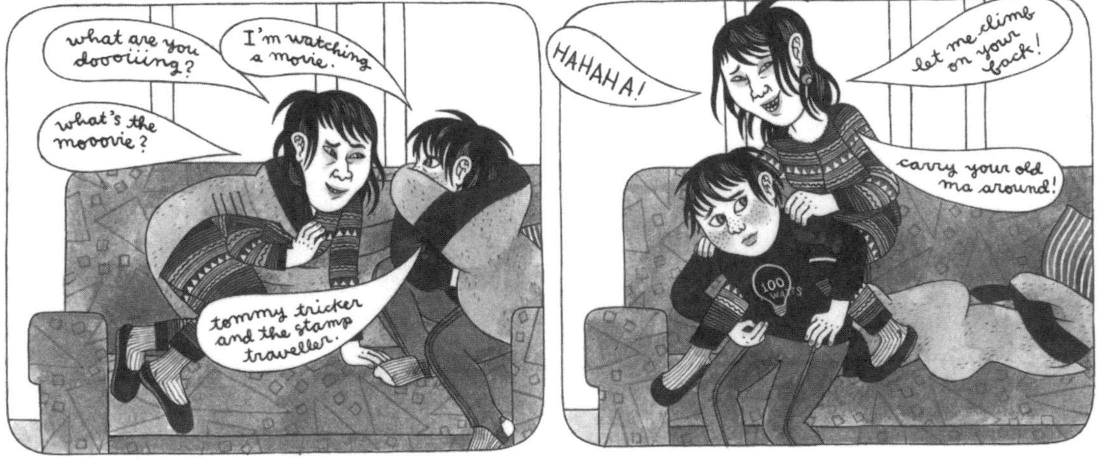
what are you doooiiing?
I'm watching a movie.
what's the mooovie?
tommy tricker and the stamp traveller.
HAHAHA!
let me climb on your back!
carry your old ma around!

I play this game with her twice in a row. The first time she finds it so funny that she runs back downstairs immediately. She is not that heavy. At ten years of age I already have big legs with super muscular calves. She wiggles on my back, pretends I am a horse. I find myself blushing from the embarrassment...

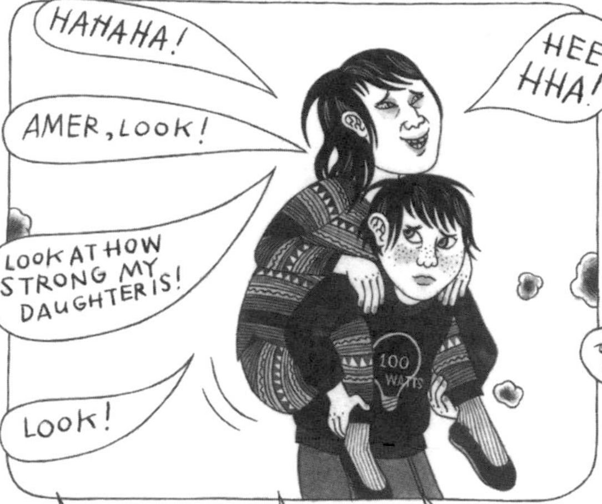
HAHAHA!
HEE-HHA!
AMER, LOOK!
LOOK AT HOW STRONG MY DAUGHTER IS!
LOOK!
100 WATTS

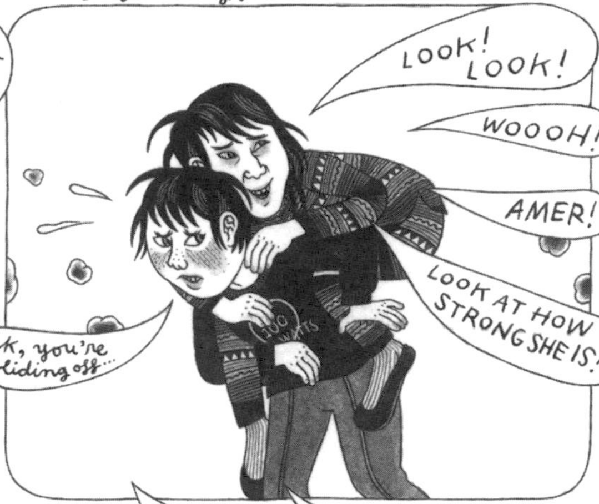
LOOK! LOOK!
WOOOH!
AMER!
LOOK AT HOW STRONG SHE IS!
ok, you're sliding off...

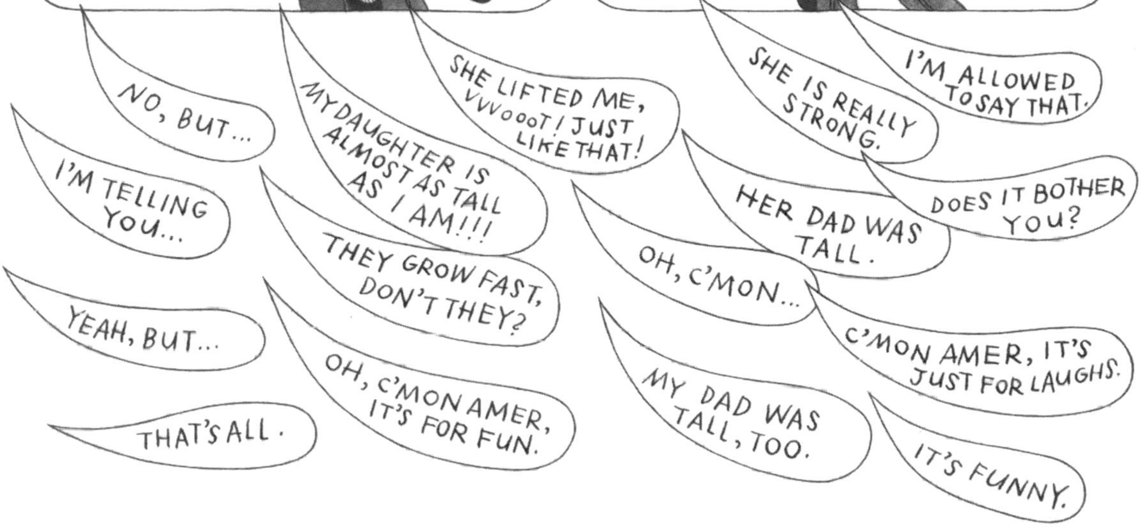
NO, BUT...
I'M TELLING YOU...
YEAH, BUT...
THAT'S ALL.
MY DAUGHTER IS ALMOST AS TALL AS I AM!!!
THEY GROW FAST, DON'T THEY?
OH, C'MON AMER, IT'S FOR FUN.
SHE LIFTED ME, VVVOOOT! JUST LIKE THAT!
OH, C'MON...
MY DAD WAS TALL, TOO.
SHE IS REALLY STRONG.
HER DAD WAS TALL.
I'M ALLOWED TO SAY THAT.
DOES IT BOTHER YOU?
C'MON AMER, IT'S JUST FOR LAUGHS.
IT'S FUNNY.

I am trying not to listen to their conversation, but I hear Amère praising me upstairs. Apparently I am going to be tall. My father and my grandfather were tall. Then Amère comes back. Does she want me to give her a piggy-back ride again? I'm really not in the mood anymore.

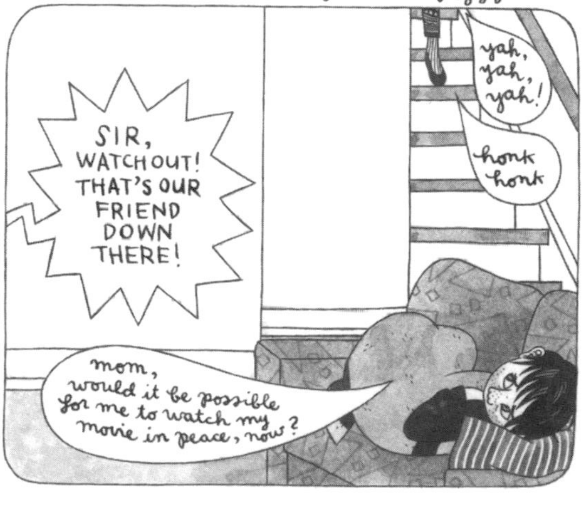
SIR, WATCH OUT! THAT'S OUR FRIEND DOWN THERE!
yah, yah, yah!
honk honk
mom, would it be possible for me to watch my movie in peace, now?

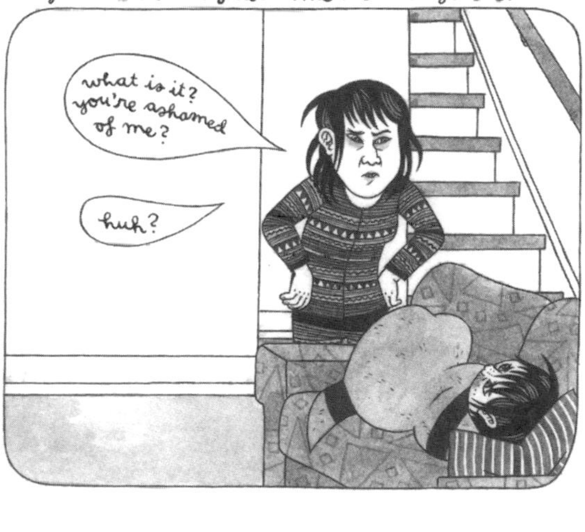
what is it? you're ashamed of me?
huh?

to drink.

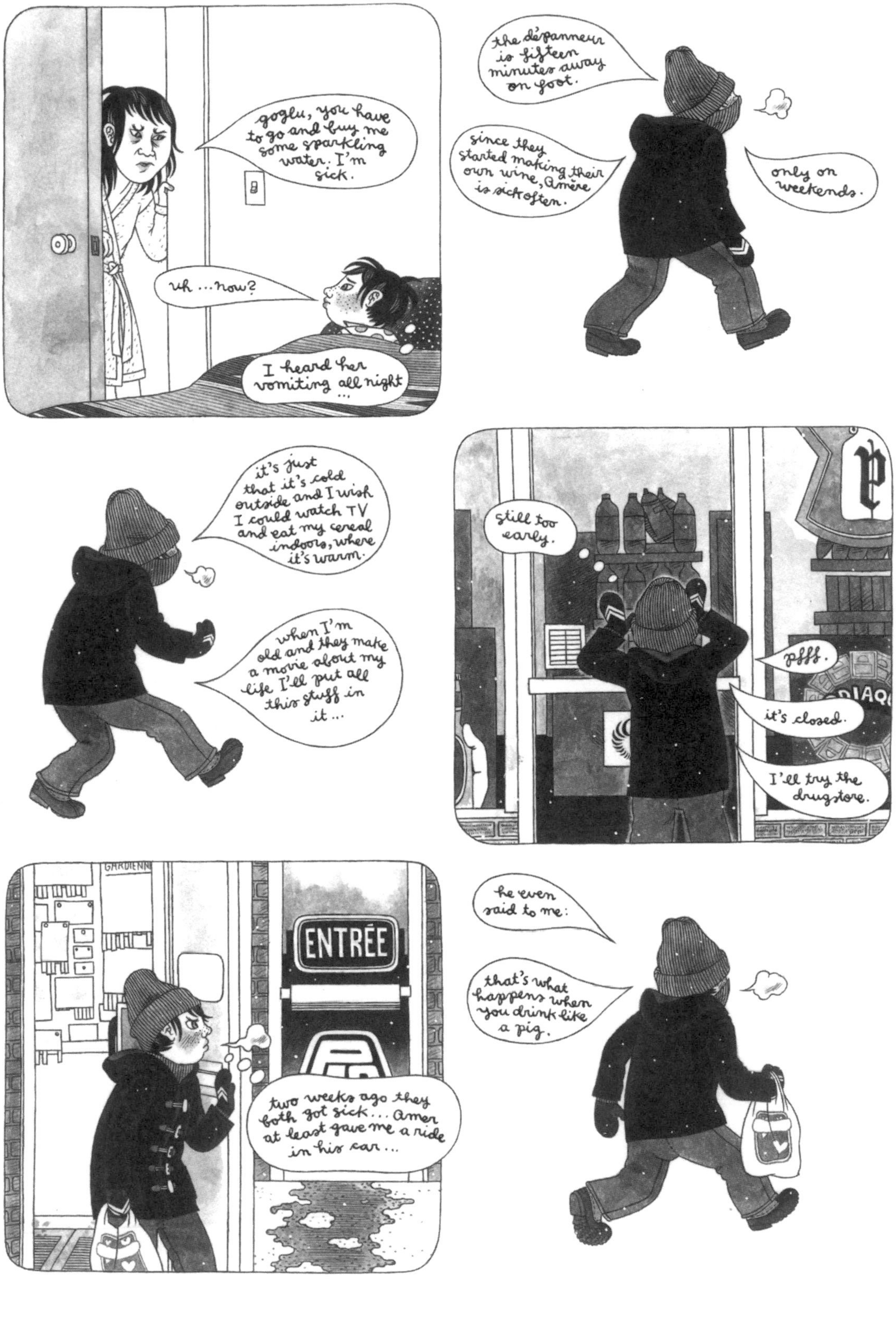
goglu, you have to go and buy me some sparkling water. I'm sick.
uh ... now?
I heard her vomiting all night ...
the dépanneur is fifteen minutes away on foot.
since they started making their own wine, Amère is sick often.
only on weekends.
it's just that it's cold outside and I wish I could watch TV and eat my cereal indoors, where it's warm.
when I'm old and they make a movie about my life I'll put all this stuff in it ...
still too early.
pfff.
it's closed.
I'll try the drugstore.
GARDIENN
ENTRÉE
two weeks ago they both got sick ... Amer at least gave me a ride in his car ...
he even said to me:
that's what happens when you drink like a pig.

my room.

Sometimes for Christmas or for my birthday, my father sends me real art supplies in the mail.

That is his only presence in my life.

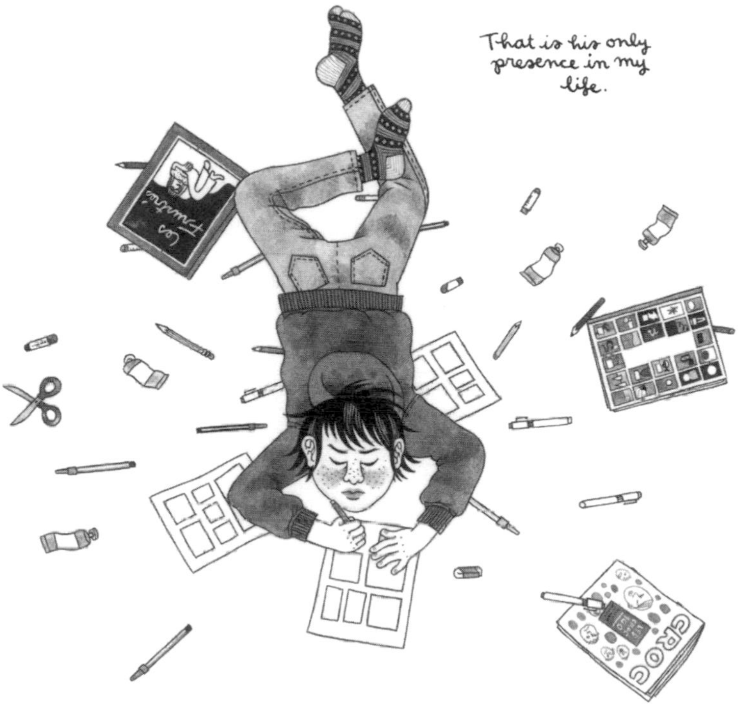
CROG

In my room I read, I build things, I make puppets with fabric scraps, but most of all, I draw.

My mom lets me do my thing as long as I put everything away at night.

eleven.

Today is my birthday ... I am turning eleven.

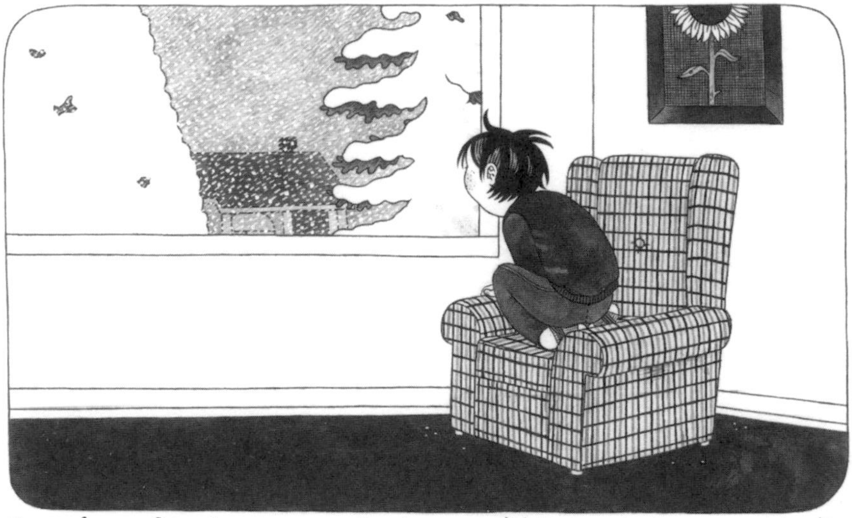

Because I haven't really made any friends yet, my mother has suggested that we invite my grandmother, my godmother, and my favourite cousin to my birthday. Amer has chosen this opportunity to visit with his daughter and brother in Sherbrooke for the night. I watch one of the last snowstorms of the season as it falls.

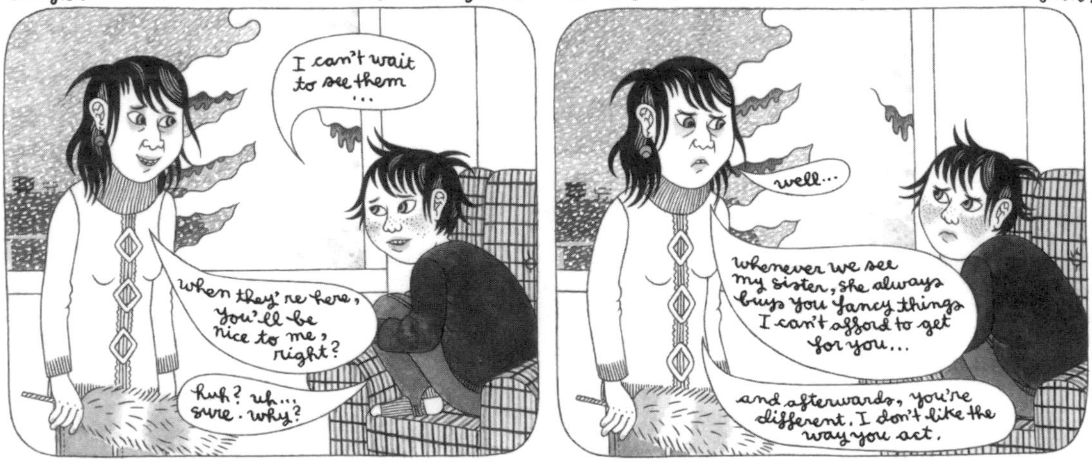
I can't wait to see them ...
when they're here, you'll be nice to me, right?
huh? uh... sure. why?
well...
whenever we see my sister, she always buys you fancy things I can't afford to get for you...
and afterwards, you're different. I don't like the way you act.

Because of the wind and snow, the roads are slippery and dangerous. Durcie, my godmother, calls to warn us that she is still at home, near Québec City. My cousin and grandmother are not coming anymore, but Durcie absolutely wants to see me. She arrives in the evening with a man who is not my uncle.

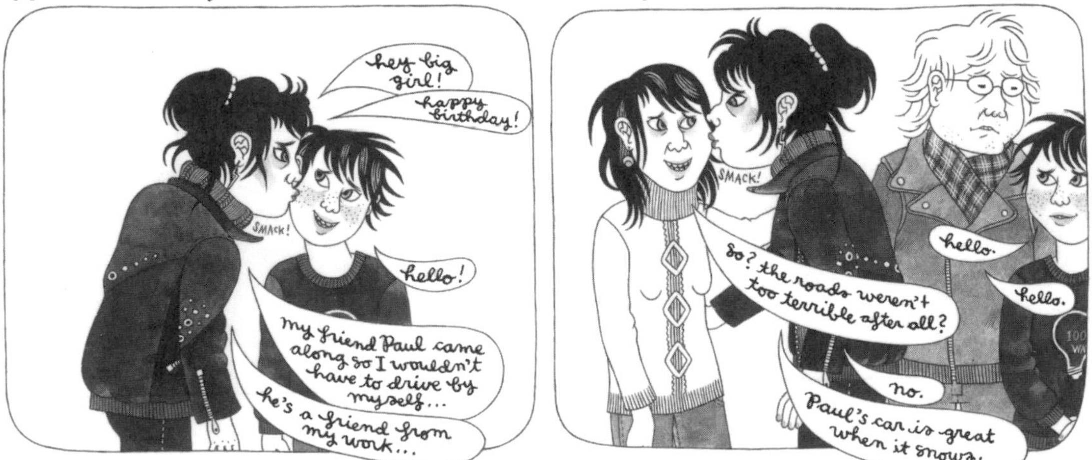
hey big girl!
happy birthday!
SMACK!
hello!
my friend Paul came along so I wouldn't have to drive by myself...
he's a friend from my work...
SMACK!
hello.
hello.
so? the roads weren't too terrible after all?
no.
Paul's car is great when it snows.

They have rented a movie and my mother has made popcorn. I wait for them in the basement. Eventually my mom and aunt start fighting, I don't know why.

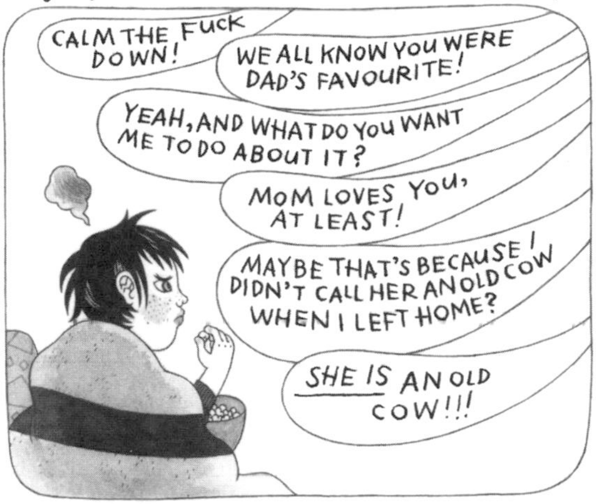
CALM THE FUCK DOWN!
WE ALL KNOW YOU WERE DAD'S FAVOURITE!
YEAH, AND WHAT DO YOU WANT ME TO DO ABOUT IT?
MOM LOVES YOU, AT LEAST!
MAYBE THAT'S BECAUSE I DIDN'T CALL HER AN OLD COW WHEN I LEFT HOME?
SHE IS AN OLD COW!!!

Paul joins me quickly. He is worried, he doesn't know how to handle this type of situation. I reassure him a little, as if I know what to do.

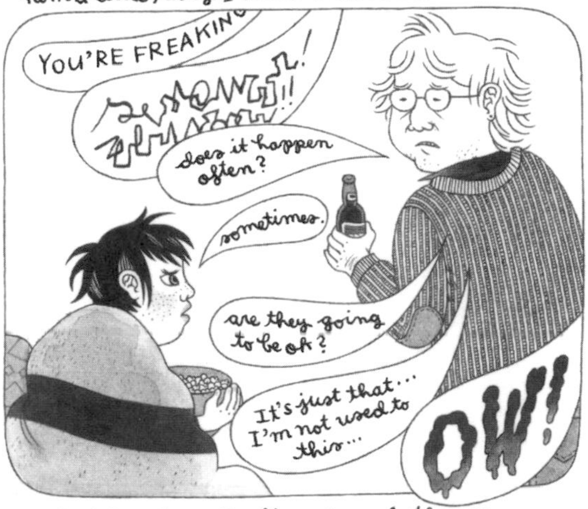
YOU'RE FREAKIN
does it happen often?
sometimes.
are they going to be ok?
It's just that... I'm not used to this...
OW!

Their screams get louder and louder. It sounds like they are hitting each other. There is a sudden loud "boom". I run to see what is happening...

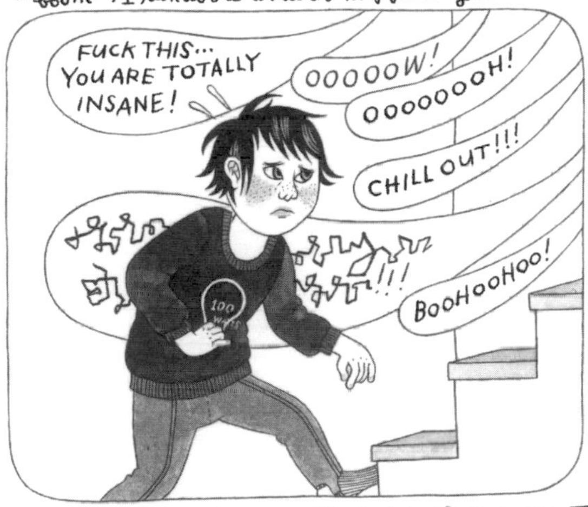
FUCK THIS... YOU ARE TOTALLY INSANE!
OOOOOW!
OOOOOOOH!
CHILL OUT!!!
!!!
BOOHOOHOO!
100 WATT

I find Durcie on the floor of our bathroom, wincing and whining. It smells like somebody has just smoked a big joint.

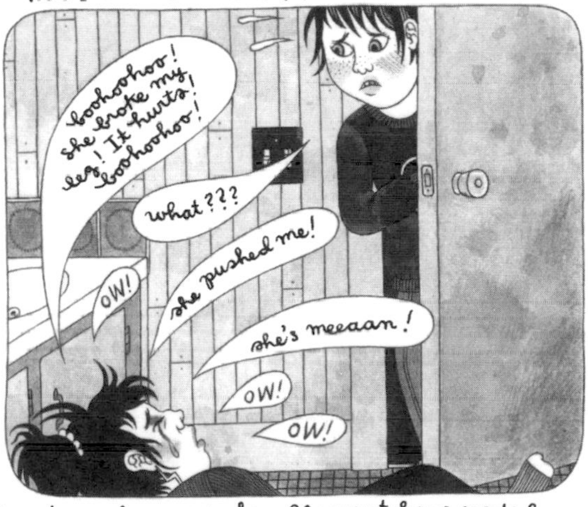
boohoohoo! she broke my leg! It hurts! boohoohoo!
what???
OW!
she pushed me!
she's meeaan!
OW!
OW!

Amère is lying down on the bed in Lu's room. There is smoke everywhere. She must have smoked a joint in there by herself... She seems completely out of it, flat on her back in the dark. Many months later, Durcie visits my grandmother while walking with a cane. Amère says she is faking it.

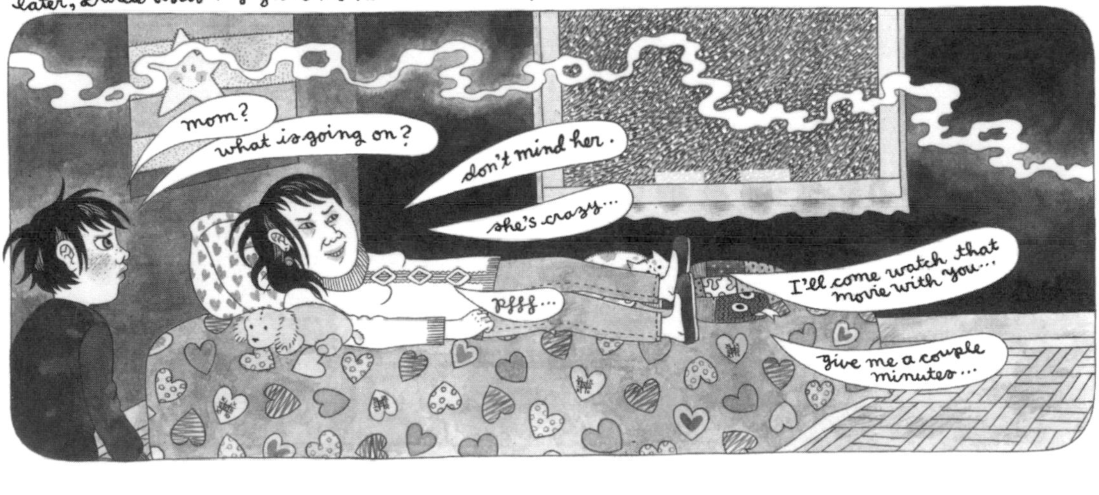
mom?
what is going on?
don't mind her.
she's crazy...
pfff...
I'll come watch that movie with you...
give me a couple minutes...

drunkard.

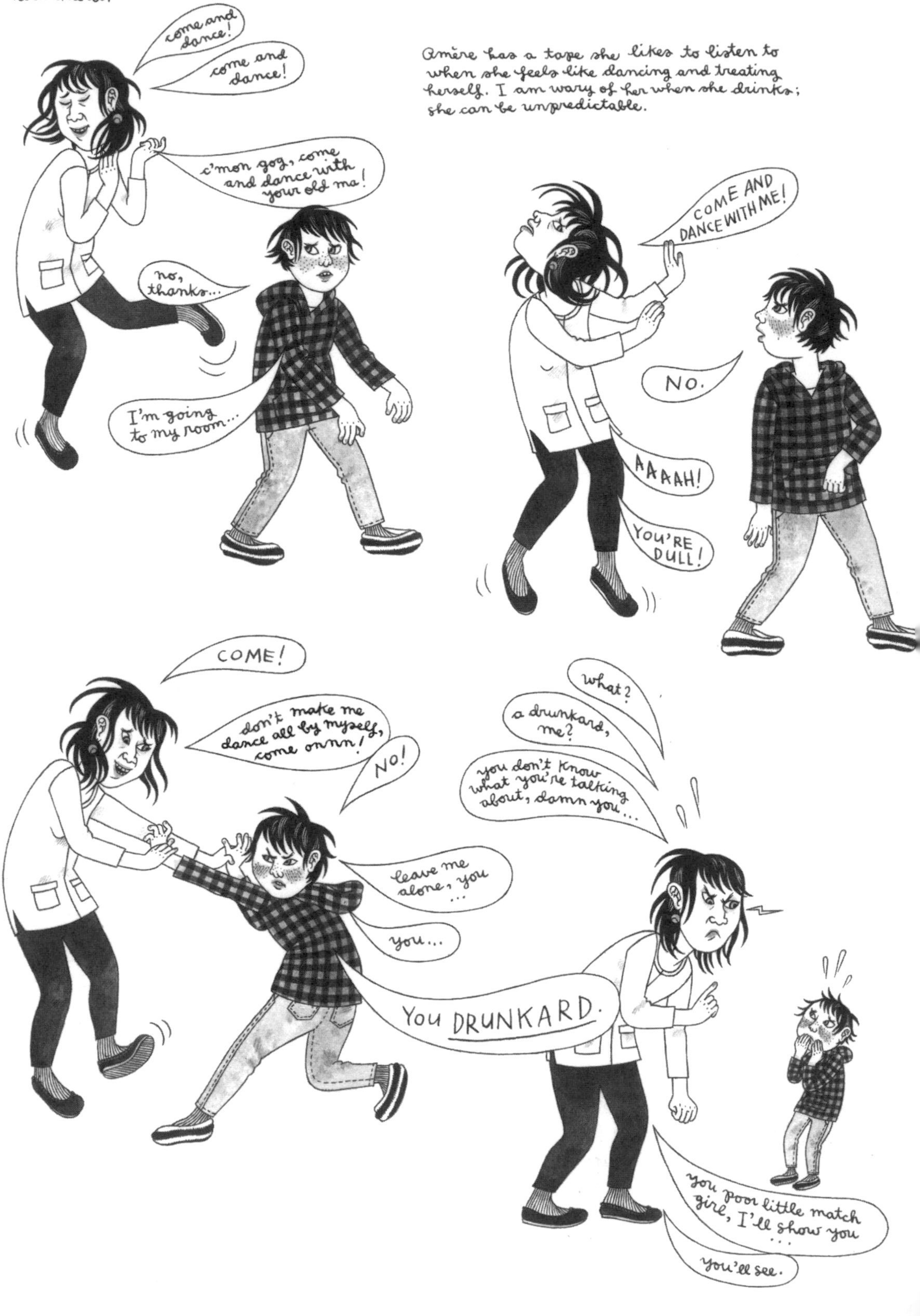
come and dance!
come and dance!
c'mon gog, come and dance with your old ma!
no, thanks...
I'm going to my room...
Amère has a tape she likes to listen to when she feels like dancing and treating herself. I am wary of her when she drinks; she can be unpredictable.
COME AND DANCE WITH ME!
NO.
AAAAH!
YOU'RE DULL!
COME!
don't make me dance all by myself, come onnn!
NO!
leave me alone, you ...
you...
You DRUNKARD.
what?
a drunkard, me?
you don't know what you're talking about, damn you...
you poor little match girl, I'll show you ...
you'll see.

punishment.

Amer and Amère come and take away my little black and white television. I am grounded for three weeks because I called my mother a drunkard last night.

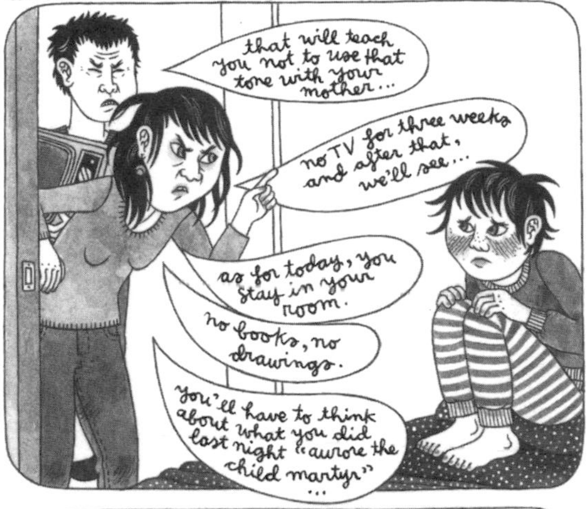

that will teach you not to use that tone with your mother...
no TV for three weeks and after that, we'll see...
as for today, you stay in your room.
no books, no drawings.
you'll have to think about what you did last night "aurore the child martyr"...

I am not allowed to do anything else but stay in bed and consider what I have done. My mother phoned my grandmother to tell her about it. Amer and Lu play a game.

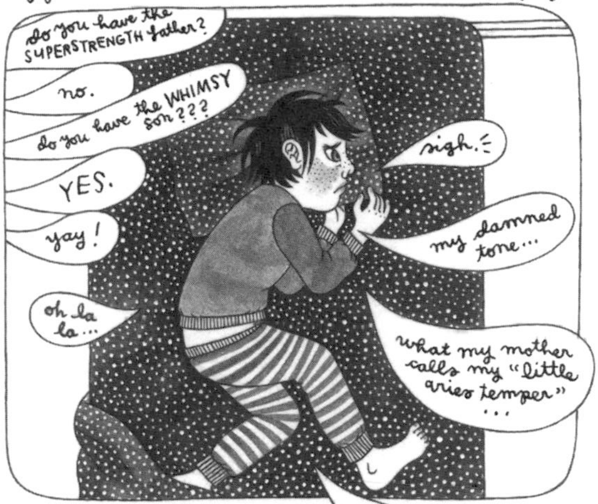

do you have the SUPERSTRENGTH father?
no.
do you have the WHIMSY son???
YES.
yay!
oh la la...
sigh.
my damned tone...
what my mother calls my "little aries temper"...
If only I could hold it in...

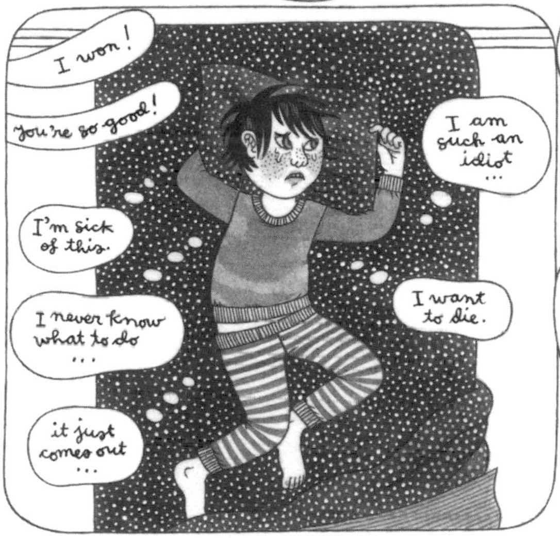

I won!
you're so good!
I am such an idiot...
I'm sick of this.
I want to die.
I never know what to do...
it just comes out...

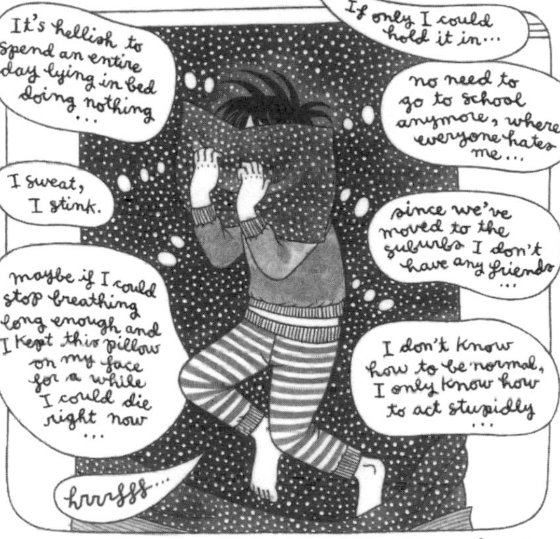

It's hellish to spend an entire day lying in bed doing nothing...
I sweat, I stink.
maybe if I could stop breathing long enough and I kept this pillow on my face for a while I could die right now...
hrrrfff...
no need to go to school anymore, where everyone hates me...
since we've moved to the suburbs I don't have any friends...
I don't know how to be normal, I only know how to act stupidly...

For at least the week following one of those moments when I disobey, I am allowed a bare minimum of conversation from my mother.

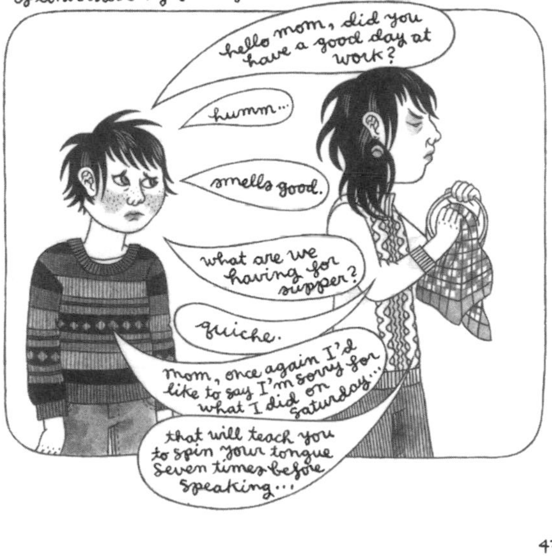

hello mom, did you have a good day at work?
humm...
smells good.
what are we having for supper?
quiche.
mom, once again I'd like to say I'm sorry for what I did on saturday...
that will teach you to spin your tongue seven times before speaking...

With Amer who mostly avoids talking to me already, the house becomes almost impossibly cold. I live alone with two accountants I no longer count on.

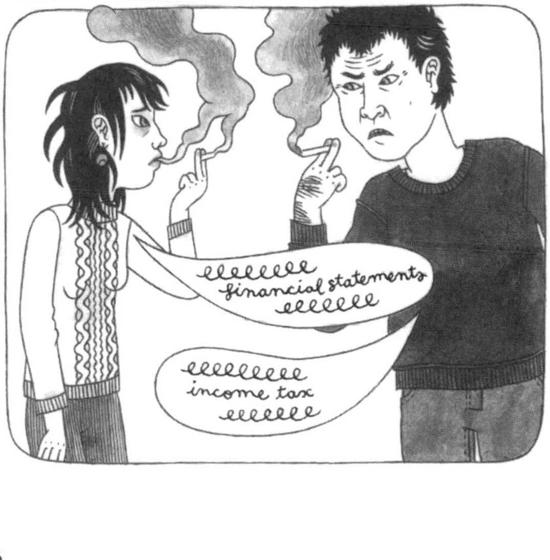

llllllll financial statements lllllll
lllllllll income tax lllllll

marginal.

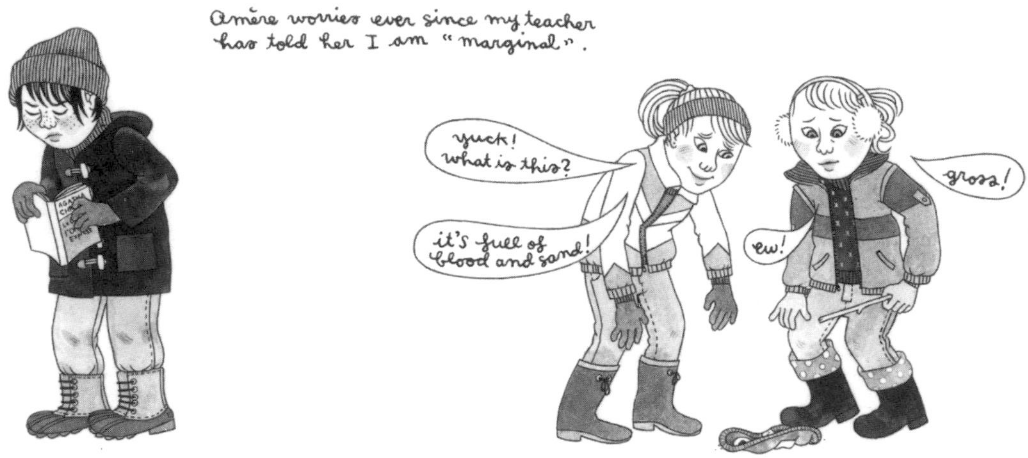
Amère worries ever since my teacher has told her I am "marginal".
yuck! what is this?
it's full of blood and sand!
ew!
gross!

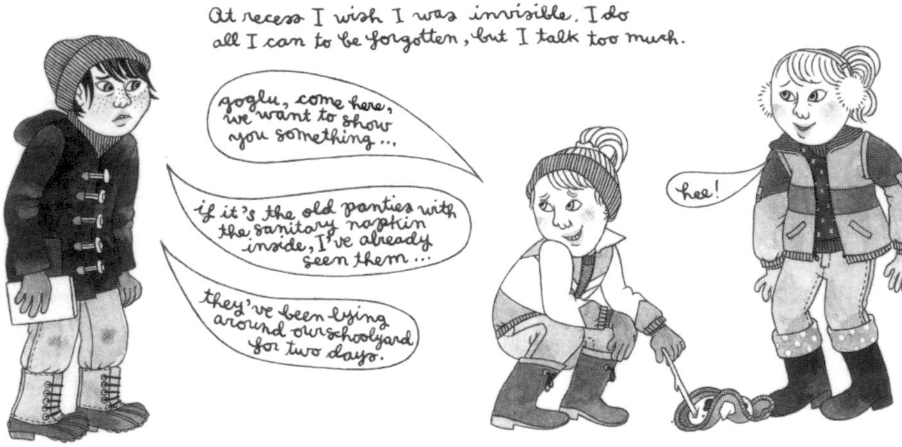
At recess I wish I was invisible. I do all I can to be forgotten, but I talk too much.
goglu, come here, we want to show you something...
if it's the old panties with the sanitary napkin inside, I've already seen them...
they've been lying around our schoolyard for two days.
hee!

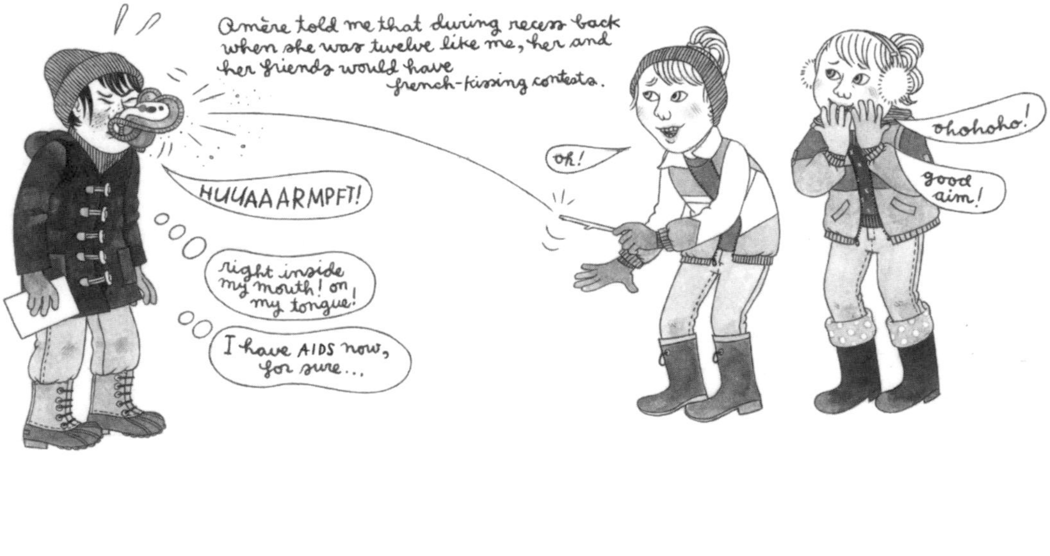
Amère told me that during recess back when she was twelve like me, her and her friends would have french-kissing contests.
HUUAAARMPFT!
right inside my mouth! on my tongue!
I have AIDS now, for sure...
oh!
ohohoho!
good aim!

Amer and I.

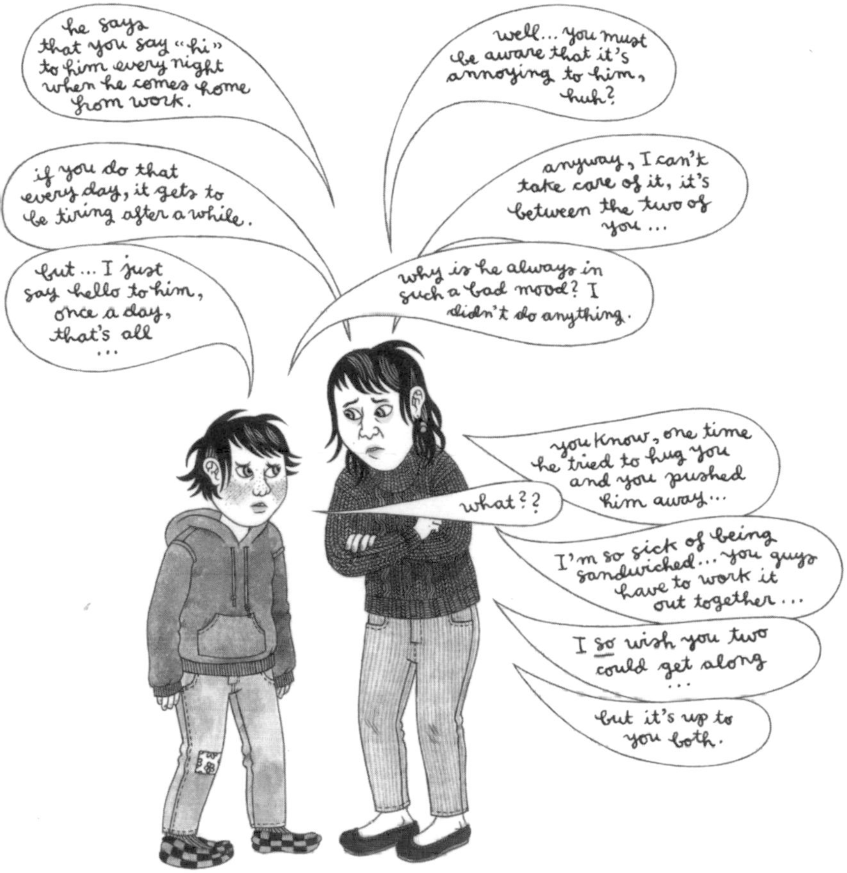

he says that you say «hi» to him every night when he comes home from work.
well... you must be aware that it's annoying to him, huh?
if you do that every day, it gets to be tiring after a while.
anyway, I can't take care of it, it's between the two of you...
but... I just say hello to him, once a day, that's all ...
why is he always in such a bad mood? I didn't do anything.
you know, one time he tried to hug you and you pushed him away...
what??
I'm so sick of being sandwiched... you guys have to work it out together...
I so wish you two could get along ...
but it's up to you both.

There is a huge argument between Amer, Amère and I. My mother feels trapped in the middle and she is crying. I decide to write Amer a letter, to calmly communicate, man to man. Amer takes my letter, looks me right in the eye and throws it in the burning fire behind him without reading any of it.

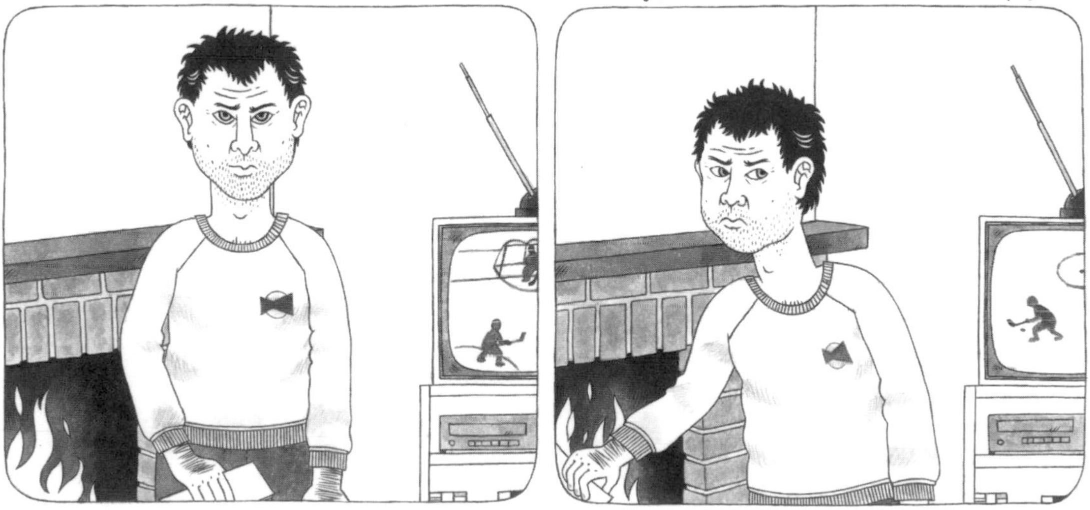

time passes.
over the next year and a half, I change.
I menstruate for the first time.

I hunch my shoulders
to hide my breasts.

friends.

I go to a school for students with better grades. Even among gifted children I struggle to make friends... just before my fourteenth birthday, I start hanging out with two girls who are sort of punk and know some older boys who live in a different suburb. I go to school with one of them.

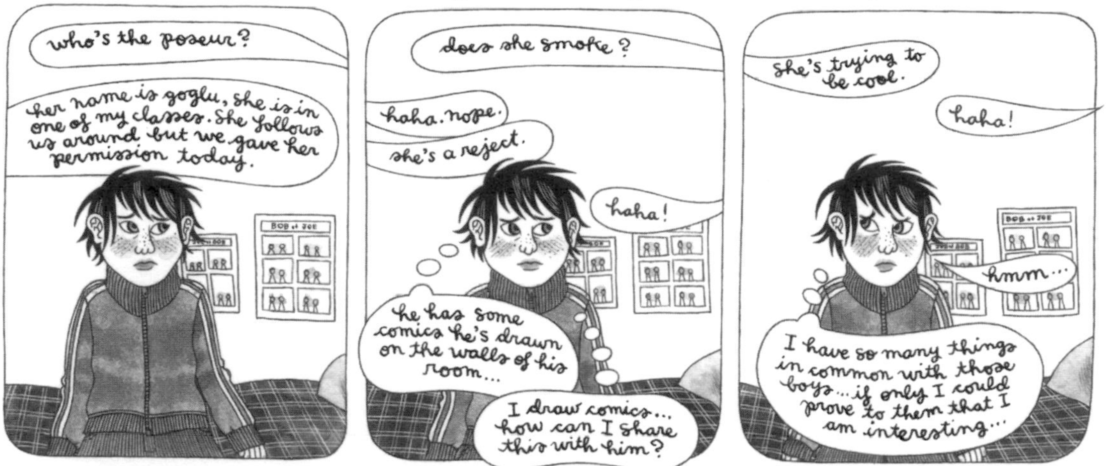
who's the poseur?
her name is goglu, she is in one of my classes. She follows us around but we gave her permission today.
does she smoke?
haha. nope.
she's a reject.
haha!
he has some comics he's drawn on the walls of his room...
I draw comics... how can I share this with him?
She's trying to be cool.
haha!
hmm...
I have so many things in common with those boys... if only I could prove to them that I am interesting...

On the night of my birthday I have permission to invite four friends, no more, to my house. Five other kids show up and I lose control of the situation. I am not allowed to use the stereo ever because one time Amer saw me turn off the TV with my big toe. When I was seven years old.

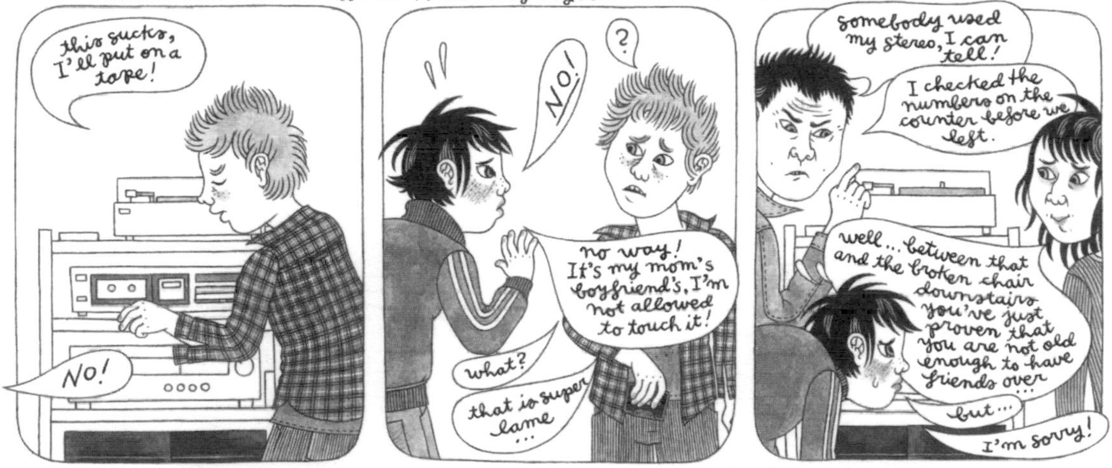
this sucks, I'll put on a tape!
No!
!!
NO!
?
no way! It's my mom's boyfriend's, I'm not allowed to touch it!
what?
that is super lame...
somebody used my stereo, I can tell!
I checked the numbers on the counter before we left.
well... between that and the broken chair downstairs you've just proven that you are not old enough to have friends over...
but...
I'm sorry!

I am very depressed. Once summer starts, I decide to write a letter to my dad in English. He replies. once school starts again, I decide that I am not anti-drugs anymore. I am taken out into the woods with an improvised bong: a glass jar with tubes. I laugh a lot. I have friends now!

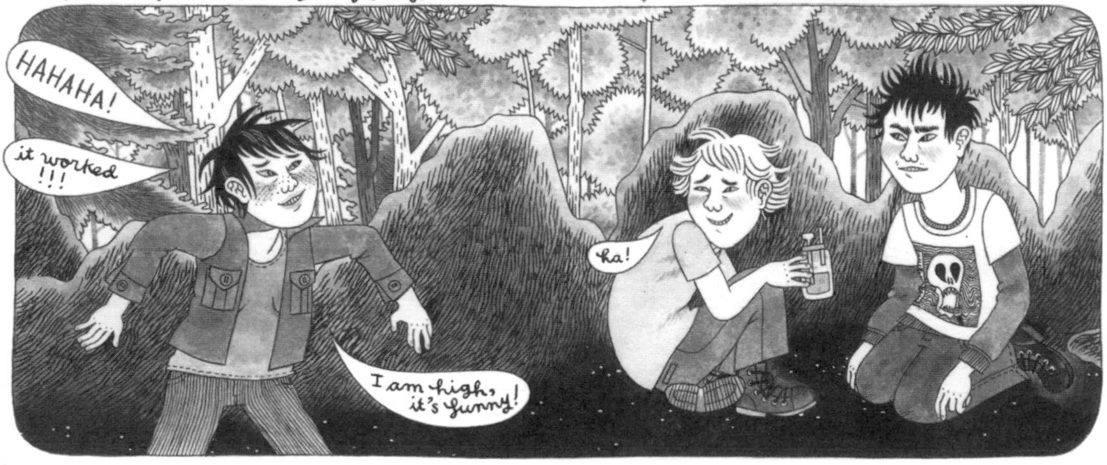
HAHAHA!
it worked!!!
ha!
I am high, it's funny!

acid.

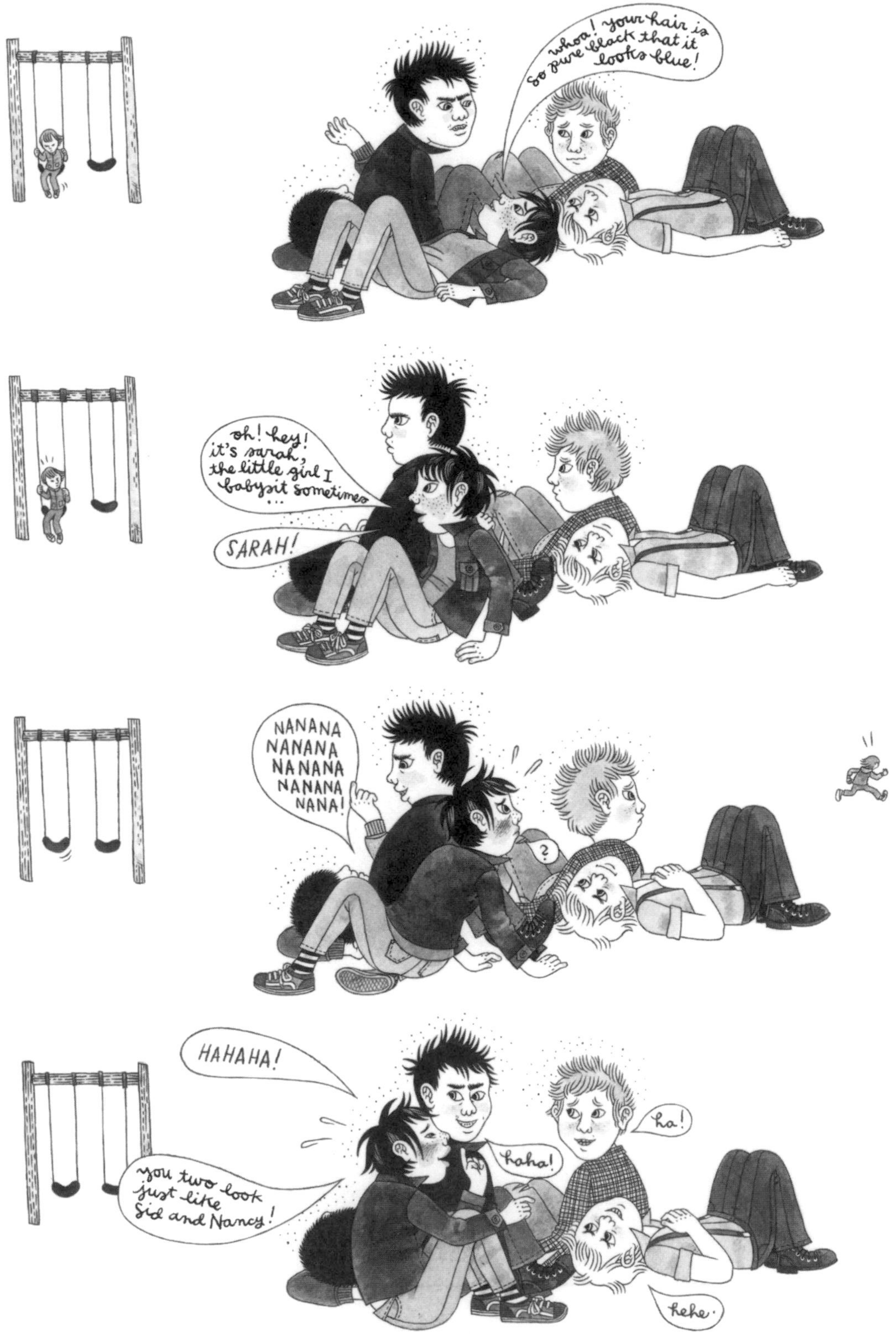

whoa! your hair is so pure black that it looks blue!
oh! hey! it's sarah, the little girl I babysit sometimes...
SARAH!
NANANA NANANA NANANA NANANA NANA!
?
HAHAHA!
you two look just like Sid and Nancy!
haha!
ha!
hehe.

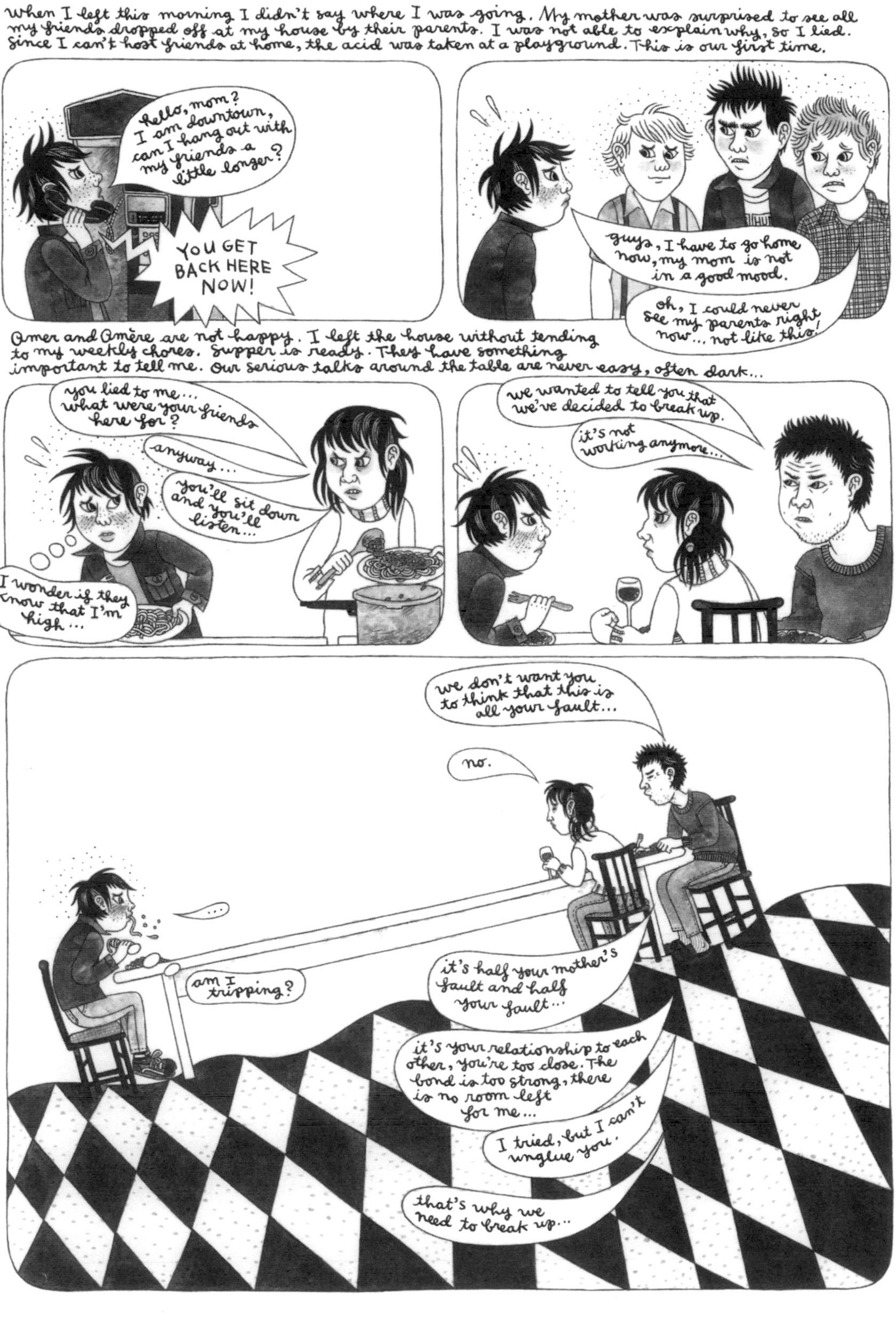
When I left this morning I didn't say where I was going. My mother was surprised to see all my friends dropped off at my house by their parents. I was not able to explain why, so I lied. Since I can't host friends at home, the acid was taken at a playground. This is our first time.
hello, mom? I am downtown, can I hang out with my friends a little longer?
YOU GET BACK HERE NOW!
guys, I have to go home now, my mom is not in a good mood.
oh, I could never see my parents right now... not like this!
Omer and Omère are not happy. I left the house without tending to my weekly chores. Supper is ready. They have something important to tell me. Our serious talks around the table are never easy, often dark...
you lied to me... what were your friends here for?
anyway...
you'll sit down and you'll listen...
I wonder if they know that I'm high...
we wanted to tell you that we've decided to break up.
it's not working anymore...
we don't want you to think that this is all your fault...
no.
...
am I tripping?
it's half your mother's fault and half your fault...
it's your relationship to each other, you're too close. The bond is too strong, there is no room left for me...
I tried, but I can't unglue you.
that's why we need to break up...

the next day I have to ask my mother:

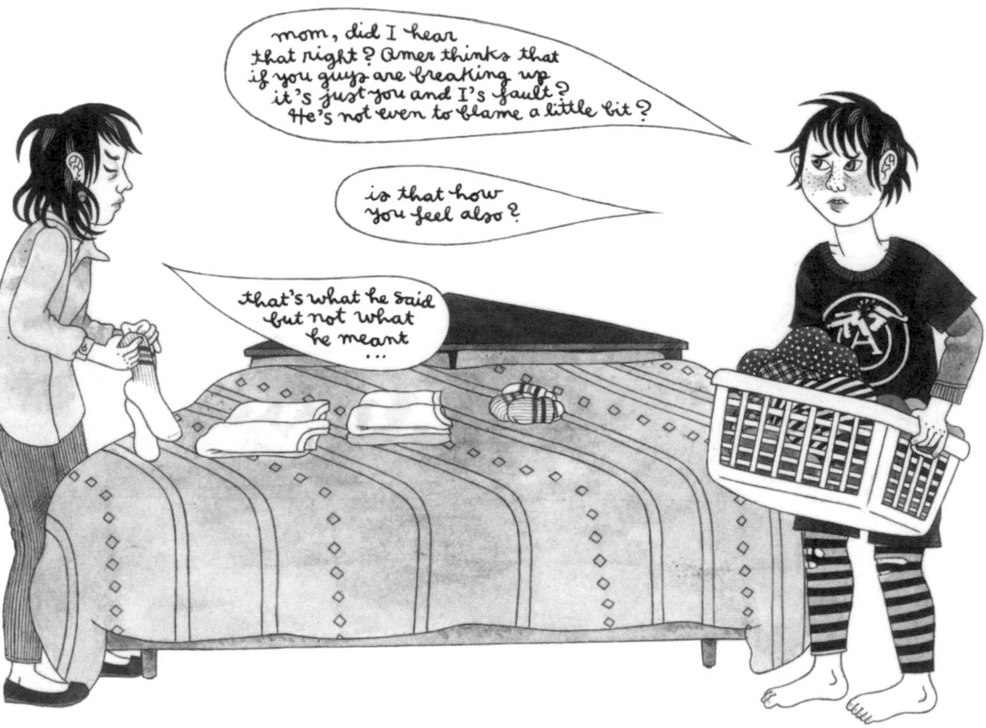
mom, did I hear that right? Amer thinks that if you guys are breaking up it's just you and I's fault? He's not even to blame a little bit?
is that how you feel also?
that's what he said but not what he meant ...

whoreslut.

I go and wait in line to see a band play with my friend Jules. We don't have tickets. I have a deal with my mother: If by midnight I find myself still at the concert, I can spend the night at Jules', in a separate room. He and I wait till the very last minute and don't get in. We go home in the snow, his mother awaits us.

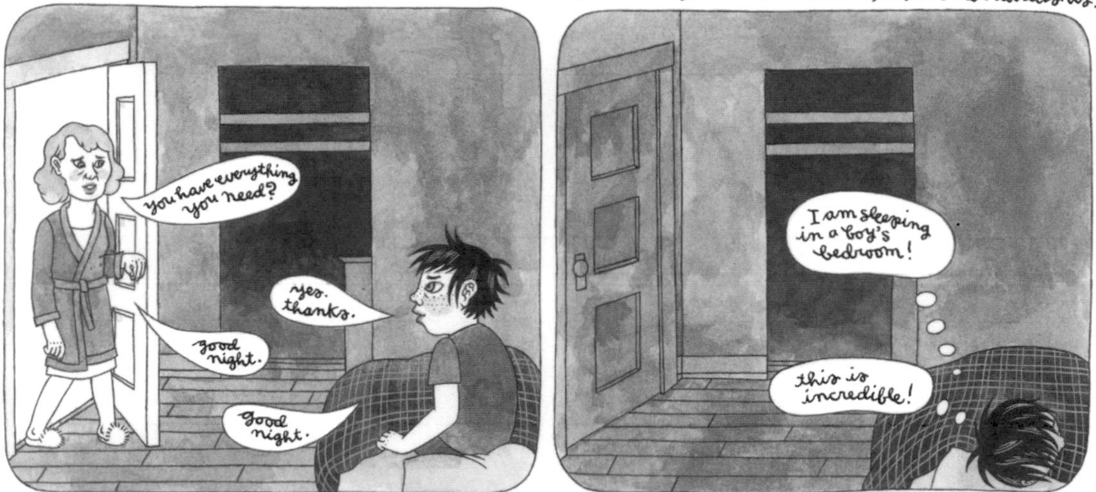

you have everything you need?
yes. thanks.
good night.
good night.
I am sleeping in a boy's bedroom!
this is incredible!

My mother learns that my friend Tom's parents are out of town. I have friends who spent the night at his house. When Amère gets angry with me she sometimes grabs the skin on the back of my neck or pulls me by the ear. She pinches hard but never hits me. When I get back today, things change.

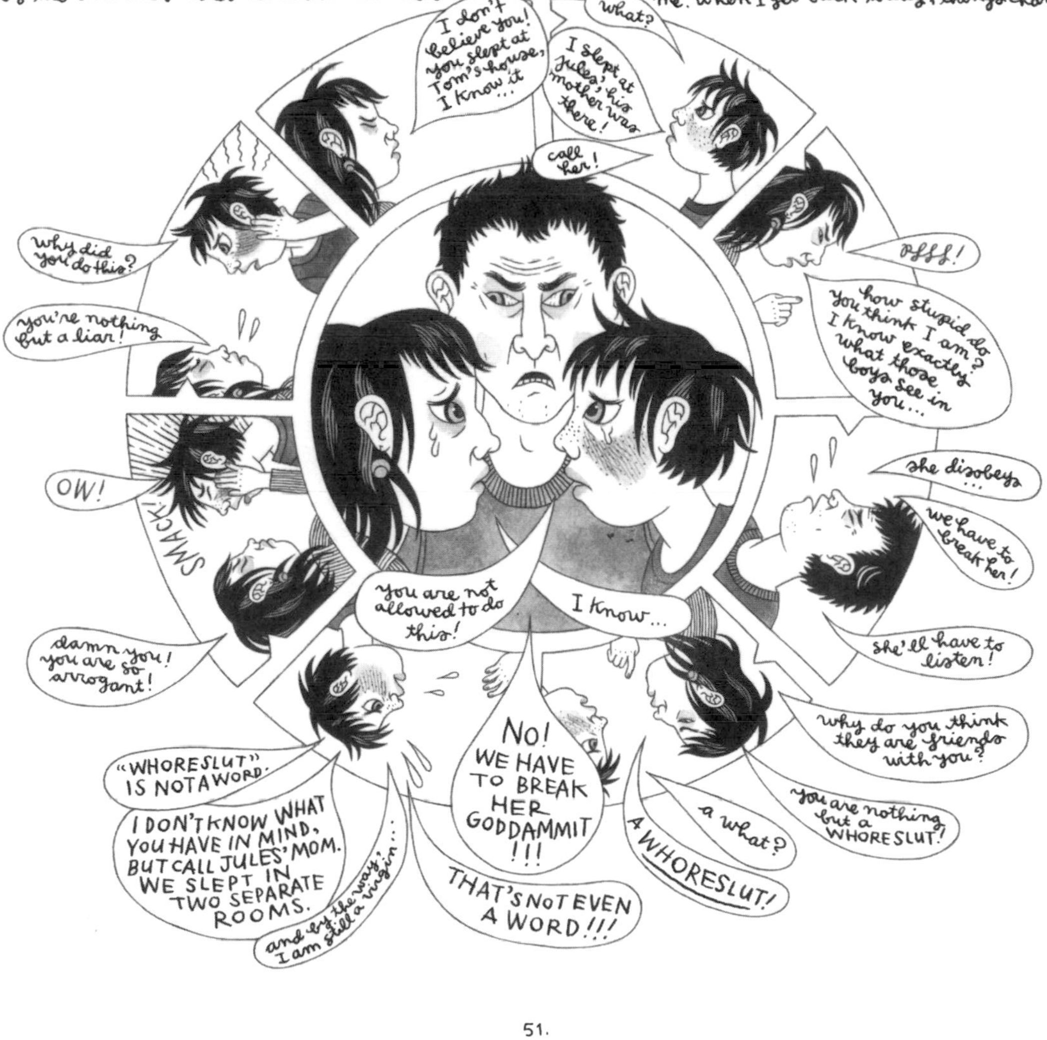

I don't believe you! you slept at Tom's house, I know it...
what?
I slept at Jules', his mother was there!
call her!
pfff!
how stupid do you think I am? I know exactly what those boys see in you...
she disobeys...
we have to break her!
I know...
she'll have to listen!
why do you think they are friends with you?
you are nothing but a WHORESLUT!
a what?
A WHORESLUT!
THAT'S NOT EVEN A WORD!!!
NO! WE HAVE TO BREAK HER GODDAMMIT!!!
you are not allowed to do this!
"WHORESLUT" IS NOT A WORD.
I DON'T KNOW WHAT YOU HAVE IN MIND, BUT CALL JULES' MOM. WE SLEPT IN TWO SEPARATE ROOMS.
and by the way, I am still a virgin...
damn you! you are so arrogant!
SMACK!
OW!
you're nothing but a liar!
why did you do this?

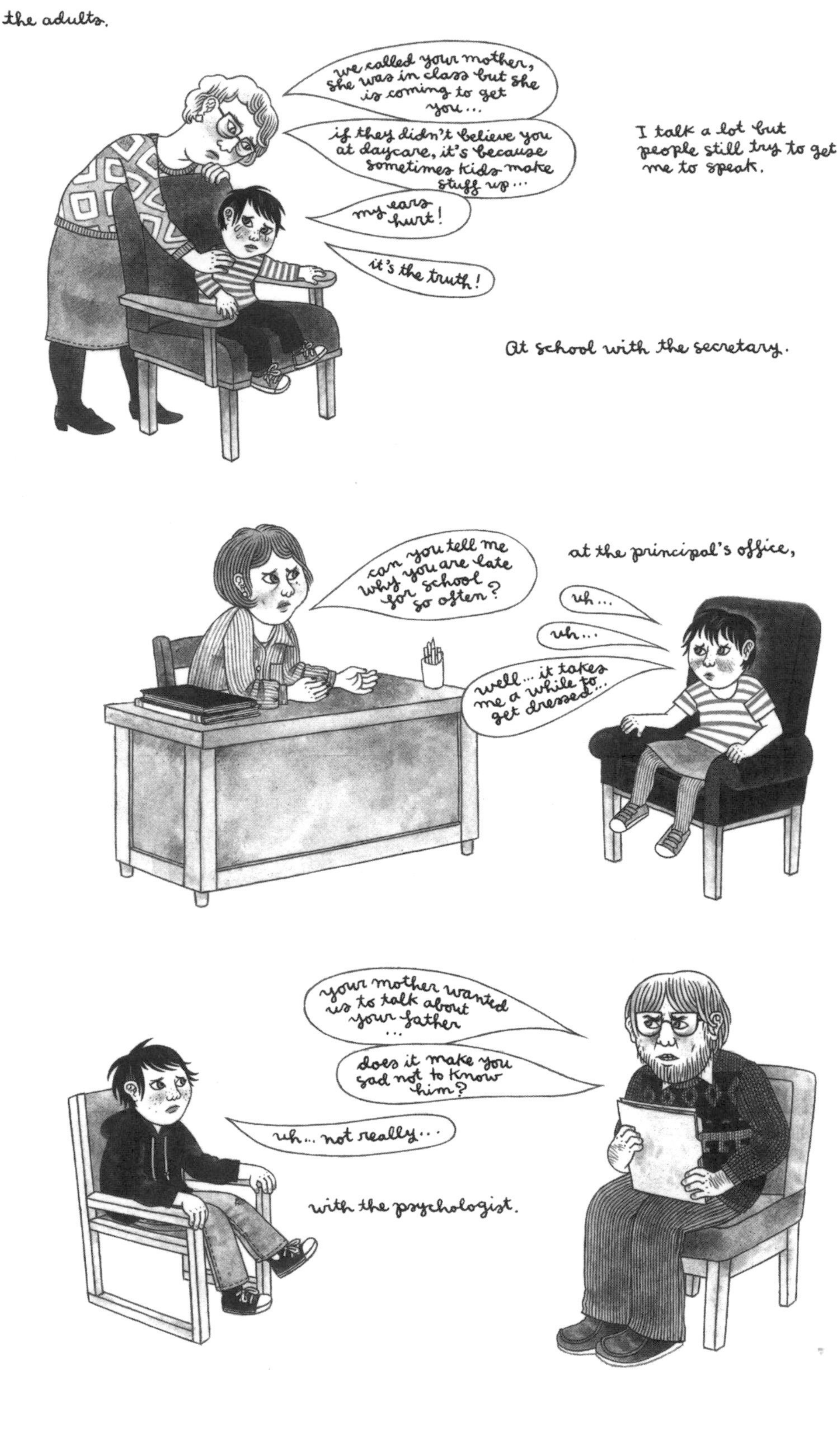
the adults.
we called your mother, she was in class but she is coming to get you...
if they didn't believe you at daycare, it's because sometimes kids make stuff up...
my ears hurt!
it's the truth!
I talk a lot but people still try to get me to speak.
At school with the secretary.
can you tell me why you are late for school so often?
at the principal's office,
uh...
uh...
well... it takes me a while to get dressed...
your mother wanted us to talk about your father ...
does it make you sad not to know him?
uh... not really...
with the psychologist.

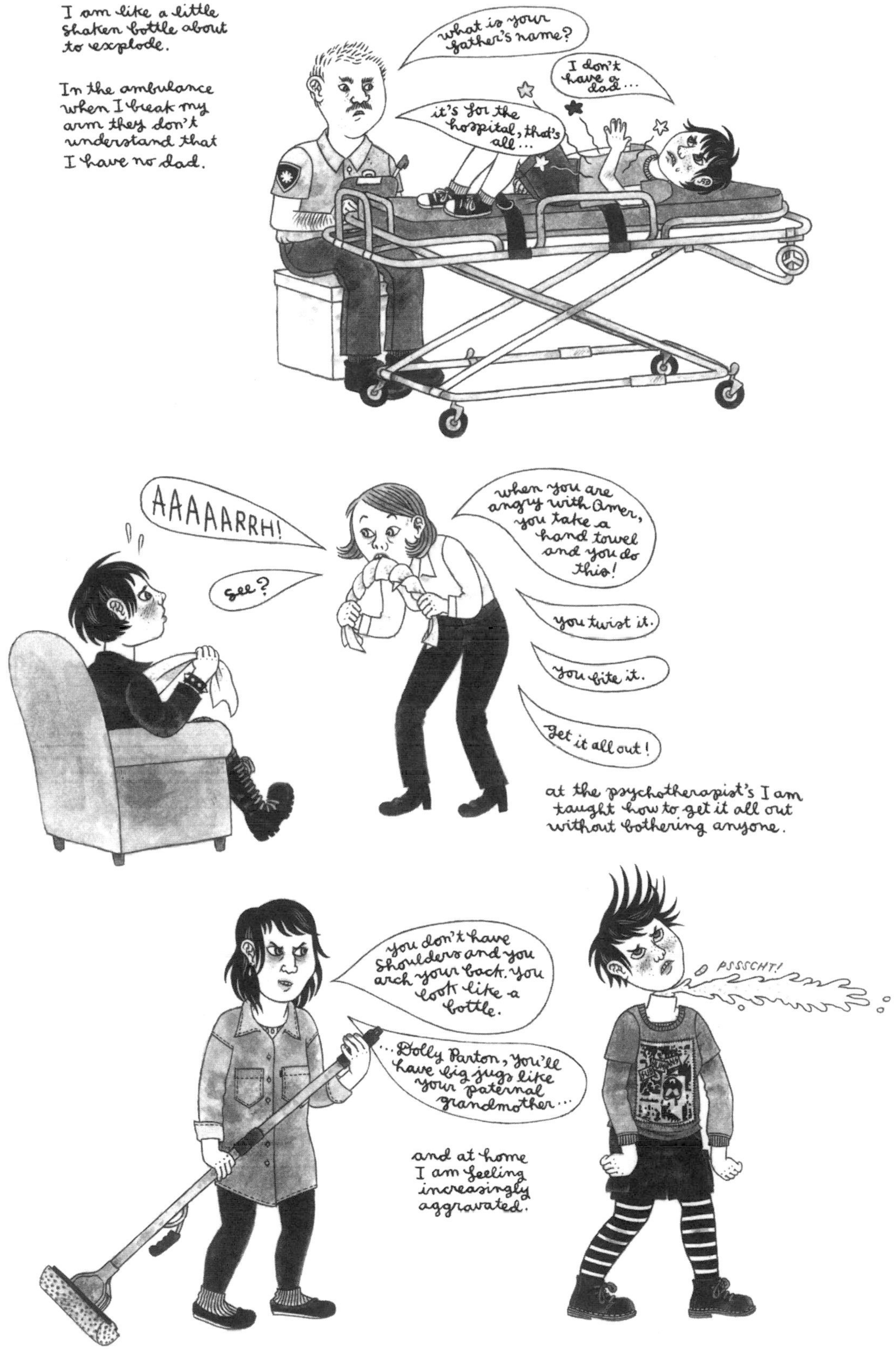
I am like a little shaken bottle about to explode.
In the ambulance when I break my arm they don't understand that I have no dad.
what is your father's name?
I don't have a dad...
it's for the hospital, that's all...
AAAAARRH!
See?
when you are angry with Amer, you take a hand towel and you do this!
You twist it.
You bite it.
Get it all out!
at the psychotherapist's I am taught how to get it all out without bothering anyone.
You don't have shoulders and you arch your back. You look like a bottle.
...Dolly Parton, you'll have big jugs like your paternal grandmother...
PSSSCHT!
and at home I am feeling increasingly aggravated.

love and respect.

you don't respect your mother. She works like a mad woman to support you and what do you give back: nothing.
See, I love your mother and I'm not going to let anyone treat her the way you do...
I bet you can't even look her in the eye and tell her that you love her ...
mom, I love you!

IT DOESN'T COUNT IF IT'S DONE ON DEMAND.
mom, I love you, you know it, I tell you often.

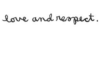

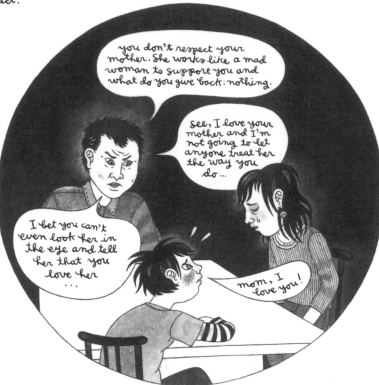

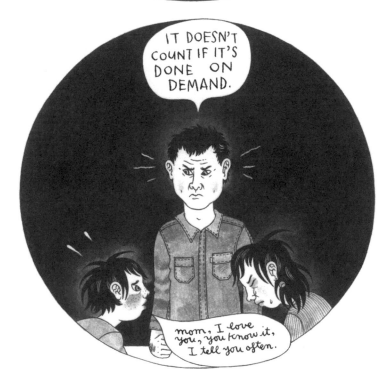

hospital.

Because I have shared with Amère that I make myself throw up, I have regular visits with a doctor and nurse.

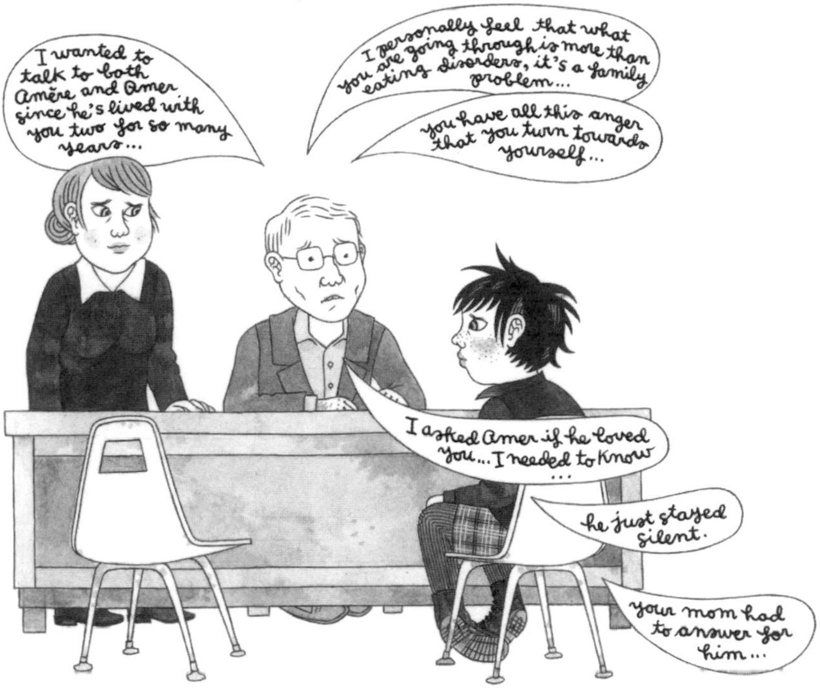
I wanted to talk to both Amère and Amer since he's lived with you two for so many years...
I personally feel that what you are going through is more than eating disorders, it's a family problem...
you have all this anger that you turn towards yourself...
I asked Amer if he loved you... I needed to know...
he just stayed silent.
your mom had to answer for him...

They listen to me, they give me advice. I cry often. At home things are not really evolving.

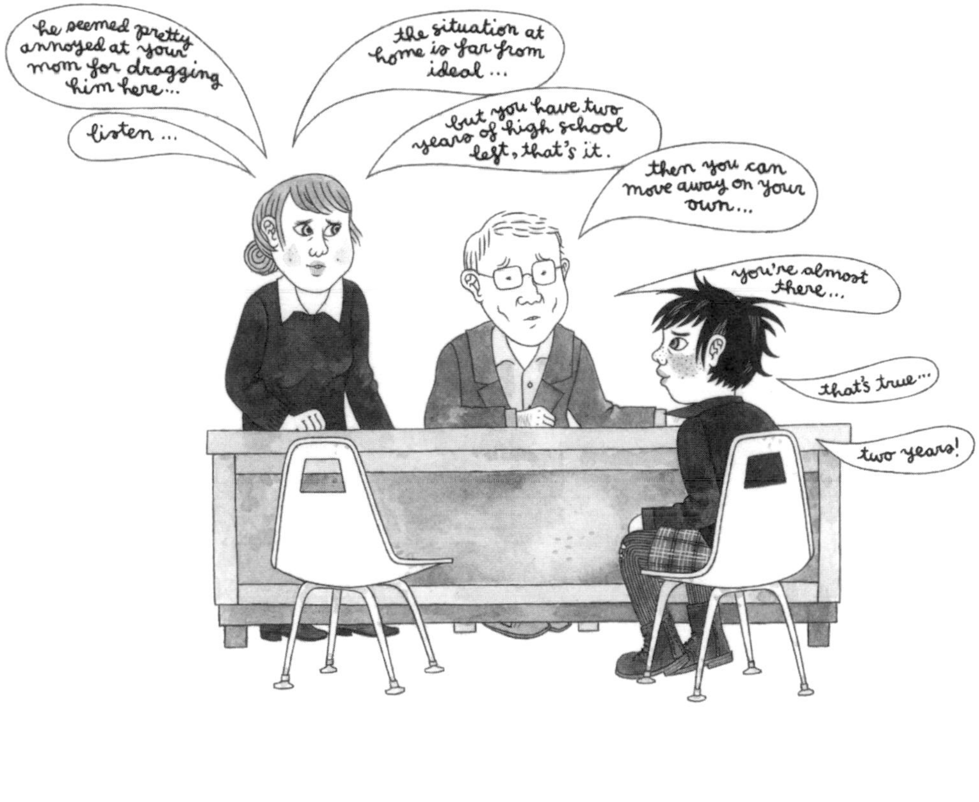
he seemed pretty annoyed at your mom for dragging him here...
listen...
the situation at home is far from ideal...
but you have two years of high school left, that's it.
then you can move away on your own...
you're almost there...
that's true...
two years!

reunion.

The doctor and nurse I have been seeing at the hospital think it is a great idea for me to visit my father. Tête d'Oeuf buys the plane tickets.

I will be spending three weeks at his place. The last time I saw him I was five years old. At fifteen, I am wondering if he will be able to recognize me.

I have a feeling he hasn't changed very much. My mother talks to him on the phone, she is describing me. I leave tomorrow morning for Vancouver.

SHE WILL BE A WEARING A WHITE HAT.

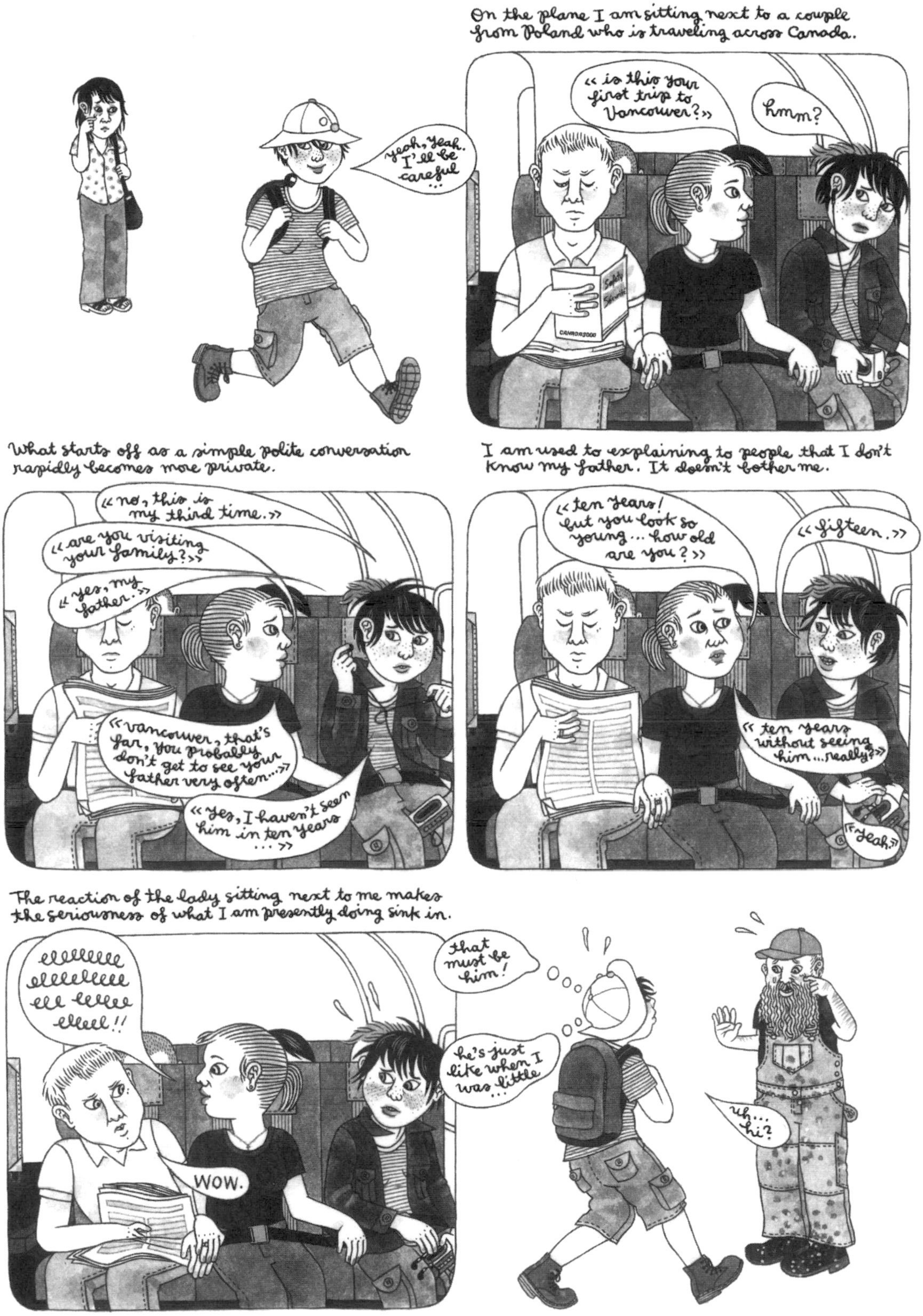

yeah, yeah. I'll be careful ...
On the plane I am sitting next to a couple from Poland who is traveling across Canada.
« is this your first trip to Vancouver? »
hmm?
What starts off as a simple polite conversation rapidly becomes more private.
« no, this is my third time. »
« are you visiting your family? »
« yes, my father. »
« vancouver, that's far, you probably don't get to see your father very often... »
« yes, I haven't seen him in ten years ... »
I am used to explaining to people that I don't know my father. It doesn't bother me.
« ten years! but you look so young... how old are you? »
« fifteen. »
« ten years without seeing him... really? »
« yeah. »
The reaction of the lady sitting next to me makes the seriousness of what I am presently doing sink in.
elllllll ellllllll ell lllll lllll!!
WOW.
that must be him!
he's just like when I was little ...
uh... hi?

He is accompanied by Sablée, his girlfriend whom he has been living with for years. I meet her for the first time and we climb in their truck.

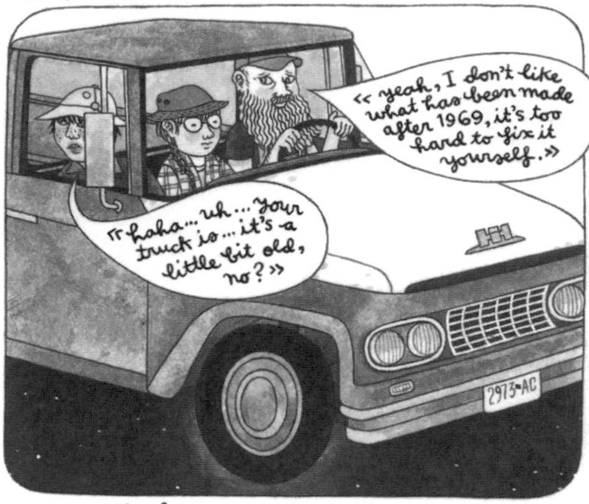
« yeah, I don't like what has been made after 1969, it's too hard to fix it yourself. »
« haha... uh... your truck is... it's a little bit old, no? »
2973 AC

They leave Vancouver Island very rarely and this big chaotic city confuses Tête d'Oeuf who freaks out. He keeps getting lost in Vancouver.

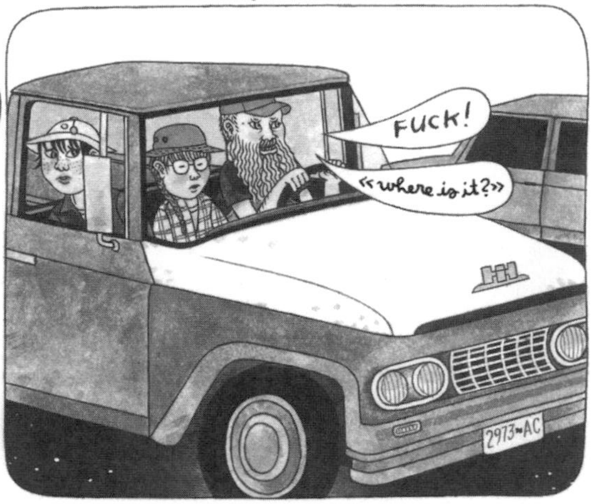
FUCK!
« where is it? »
2973 AC

Once on the ferry, Tête d'Oeuf and I hang out on the deck where cars are parked. I am uncomfortable and I can tell that he is nervous as well...

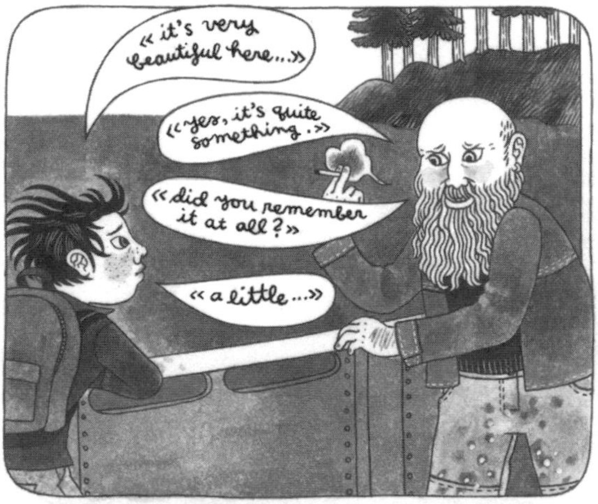
« it's very beautiful here... »
« yes, it's quite something. »
« did you remember it at all? »
« a little... »

My father is a housepainter. He has this idea about making me work with him. It should keep us busy throughout our shared malaise.

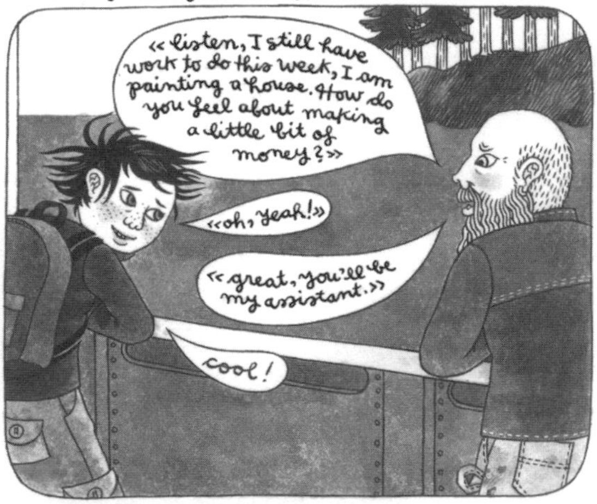
« listen, I still have work to do this week, I am painting a house. How do you feel about making a little bit of money? »
« oh, yeah! »
« great, you'll be my assistant. »
cool!

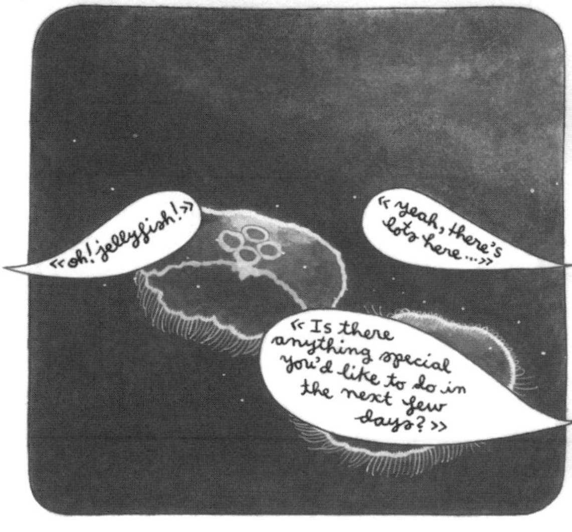
« oh! jellyfish! »
« yeah, there's lots here... »
« Is there anything special you'd like to do in the next few days? »

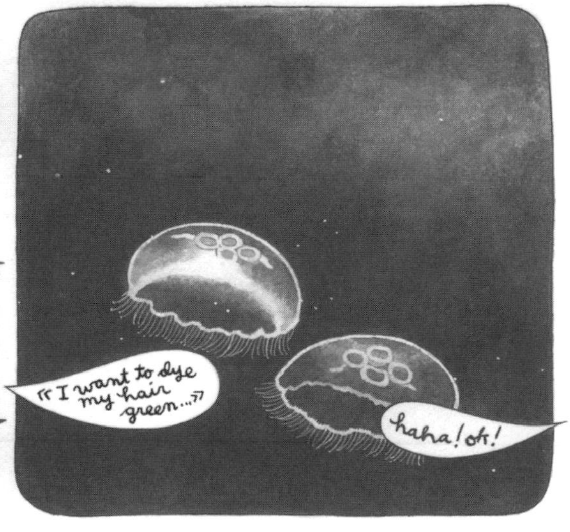
« I want to dye my hair green... »
haha! ok!

The trip on the ferry takes an hour and a half. Once we arrive on Vancouver Island we have to drive about an hour before we get to Tête d'Oeuf and Sablée's house. The scenery is magnificent. A bay, hills, a million trees. The road goes deeper and deeper into the woods.

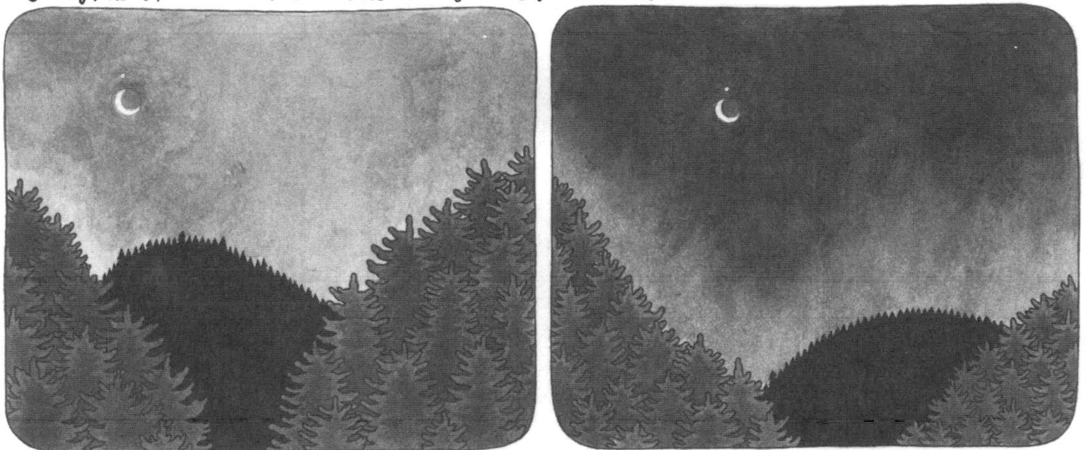

They have built their house themselves with materials and pieces recycled from historical houses around the region. The house is in the shadow of giant firs. It always feels slightly cold inside. My father has nailed a blanket to the ceiling to make a wall for me.

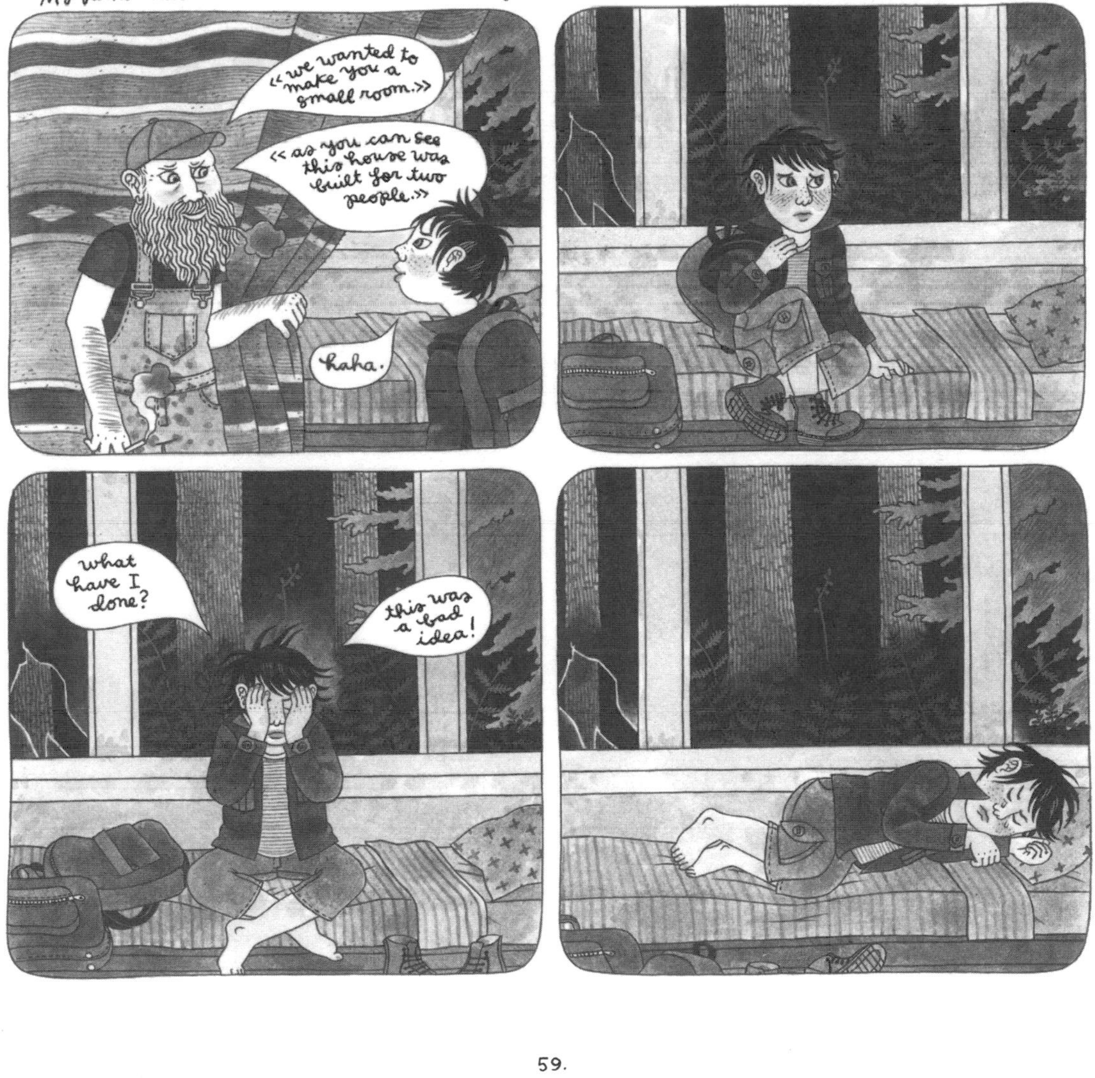

«we wanted to make you a small room.»
«as you can see this house was built for two people.»
haha.
what have I done?
this was a bad idea!

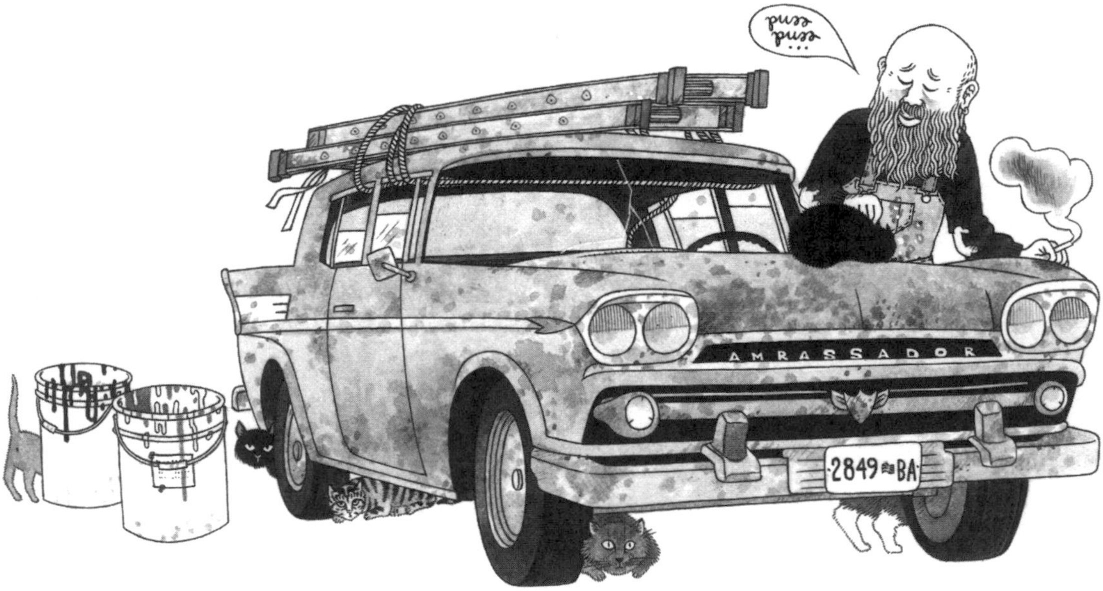
puss
puss
...
AMBASSADOR
2849 BA

Sablée is really nice. I was expecting our first encounter to be difficult, but it has not been at all. She is shy and serious, yet together we have fascinating conversations. She is very curious, which is a trait I am always attracted to in people. She is a carpenter and she works with strong-willed women.

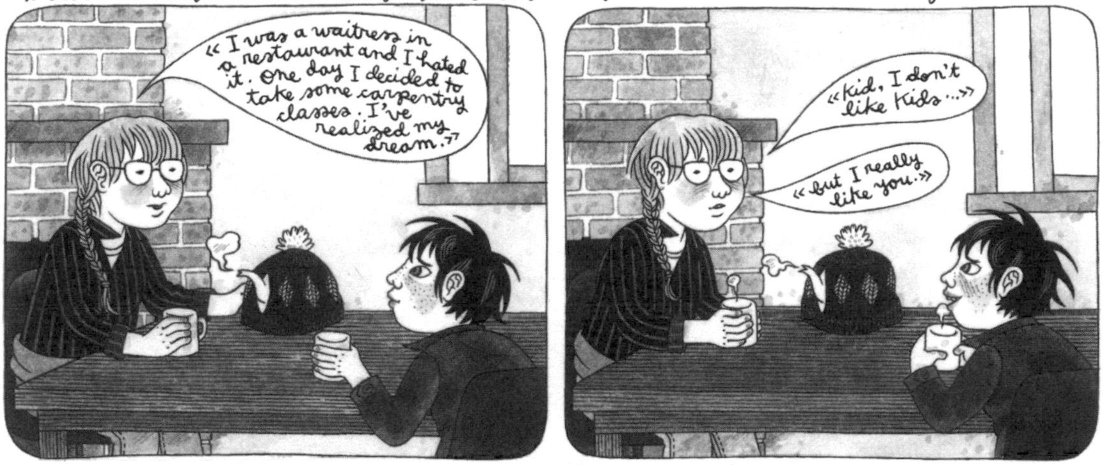
« I was a waitress in a restaurant and I hated it. One day I decided to take some carpentry classes. I've realized my dream. »
« Kid, I don't like kids... »
« but I really like you. »

Tête d'Oeuf and Sablée live with twelve cats and three or four other strays who hang around sometimes. Three of the cats sleep with them every night and in the winter all the other cats fight to sleep in the warmth of their bed. It can be overwhelming, but I like cats.

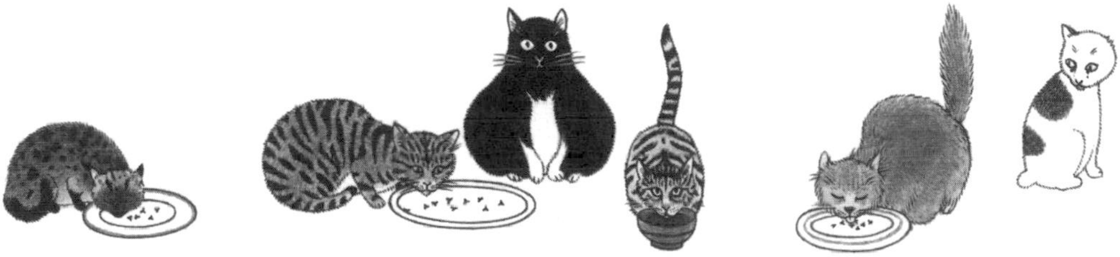

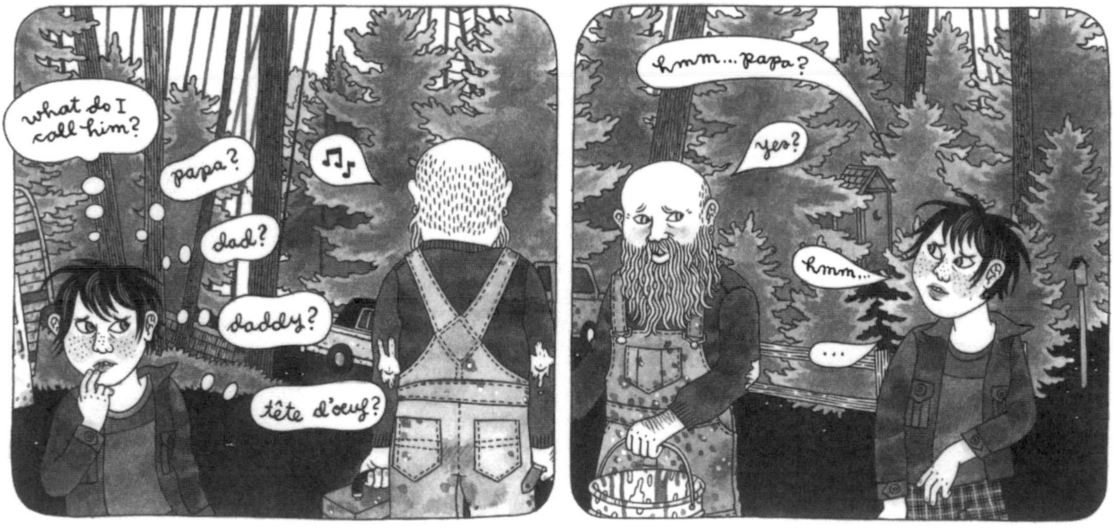
what do I call him?
papa?
dad?
daddy?
tête d'oeuf?
hmm... papa?
yes?
hmm...
...

victoria II.

It is the weekend and Tête d'Oeuf brings me to Victoria to visit some friends who are having a birthday party for their little girl. There are kids everywhere and a dog tied to a rope is sweating in the yard. Some of the ladies are very excited to talk to me, they give me hard cider.

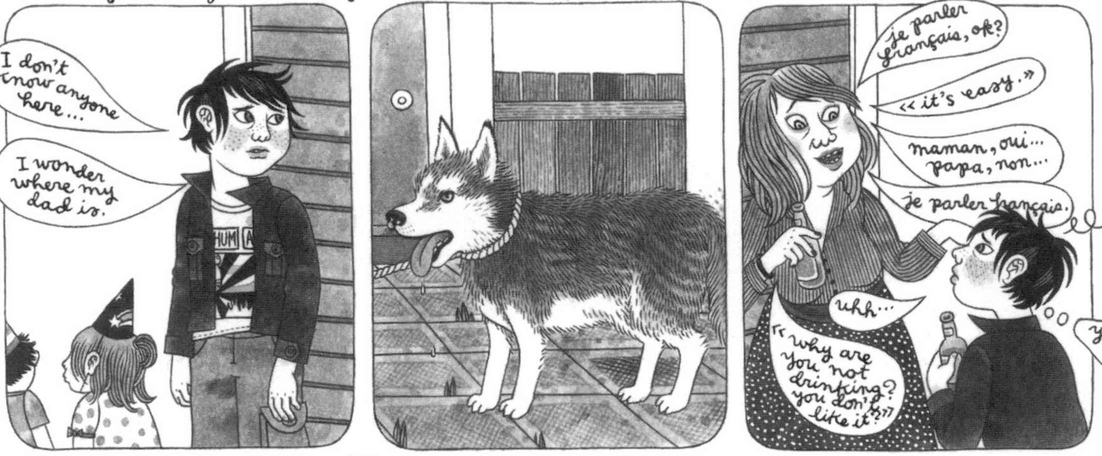
I don't know anyone here...
I wonder where my dad is.
je parler français, ok?
« it's easy. »
maman, oui... papa, non...
je parler français.
uhh...
« why are you not drinking? you don't like it? »
yuck.

I am not used to drinking and I am instantly drunk. I look for my father in the house and I finally find him in the attic with some men I've never met who must be the friends he told me about, the ones whose records I own. There is also a weird older man sitting in that room.

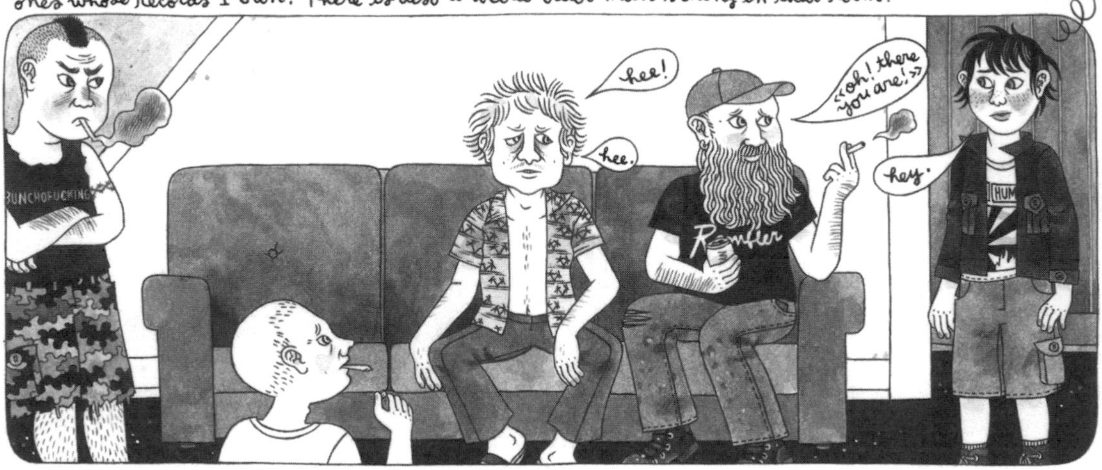
hee!
hee.
« oh! there you are! »
hey.

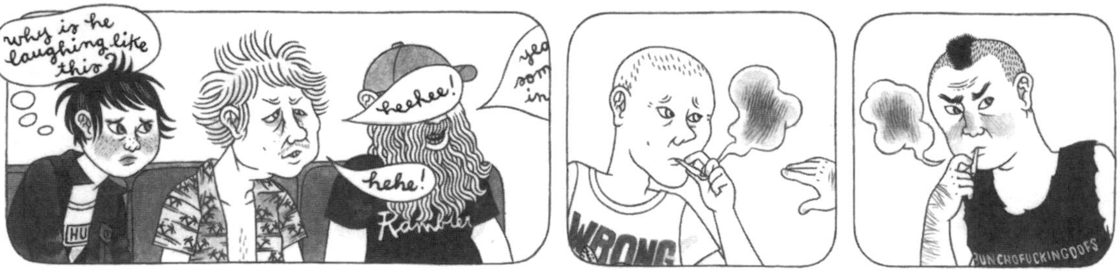
why is he laughing like this?
heehee!
hehe!

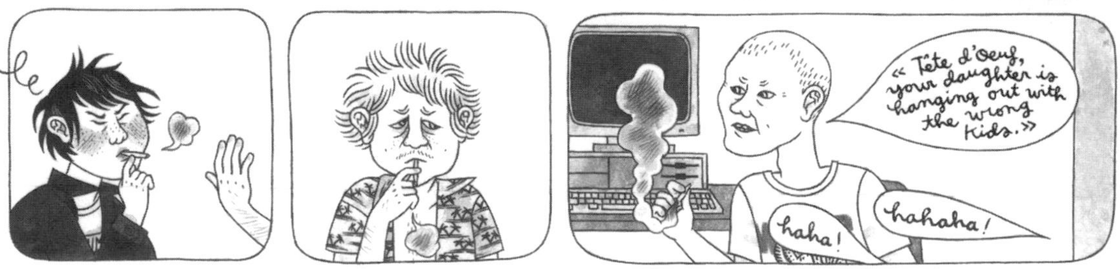
« Tête d'Oeuf, your daughter is hanging out with the wrong kids. »
haha!
hahaha!

High as a kite, I have a hard time standing up and everything seems funny. It is getting harder and harder to speak English but I intend to impress everyone. When I am passed a beer, I drink it. When I am passed a joint, I smoke it. I agree with everything that is said and done.

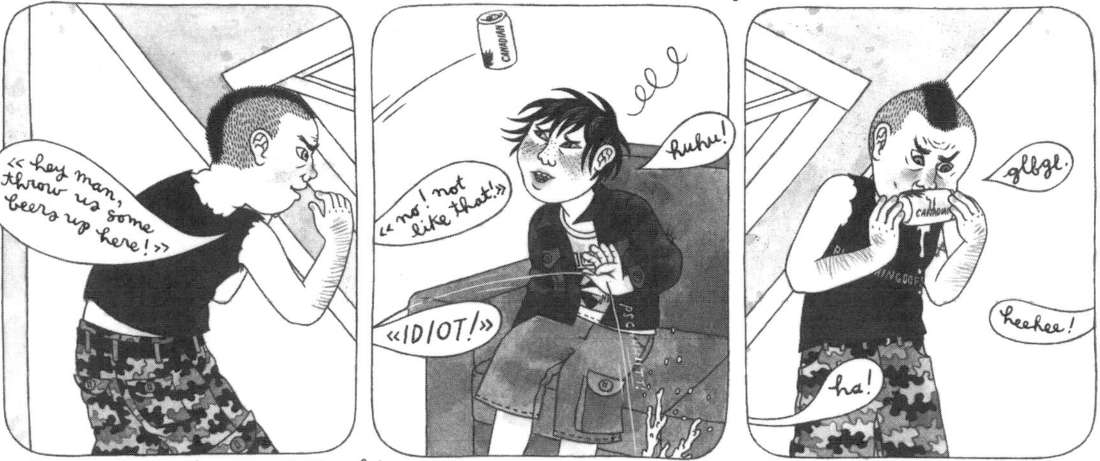
« hey man, throw us some beers up here! »
CANADIAN
« no! not like that! »
huhu!
«IDIOT!»
glbgl.
heehee!
ha!

Late in the evening my father drives us back to his place. He admits that Sablée stayed home because she is not very fond of those people. He tells me that the last time they were over at his house they broke a window in the room where I sleep, a window which has yet to be fixed.

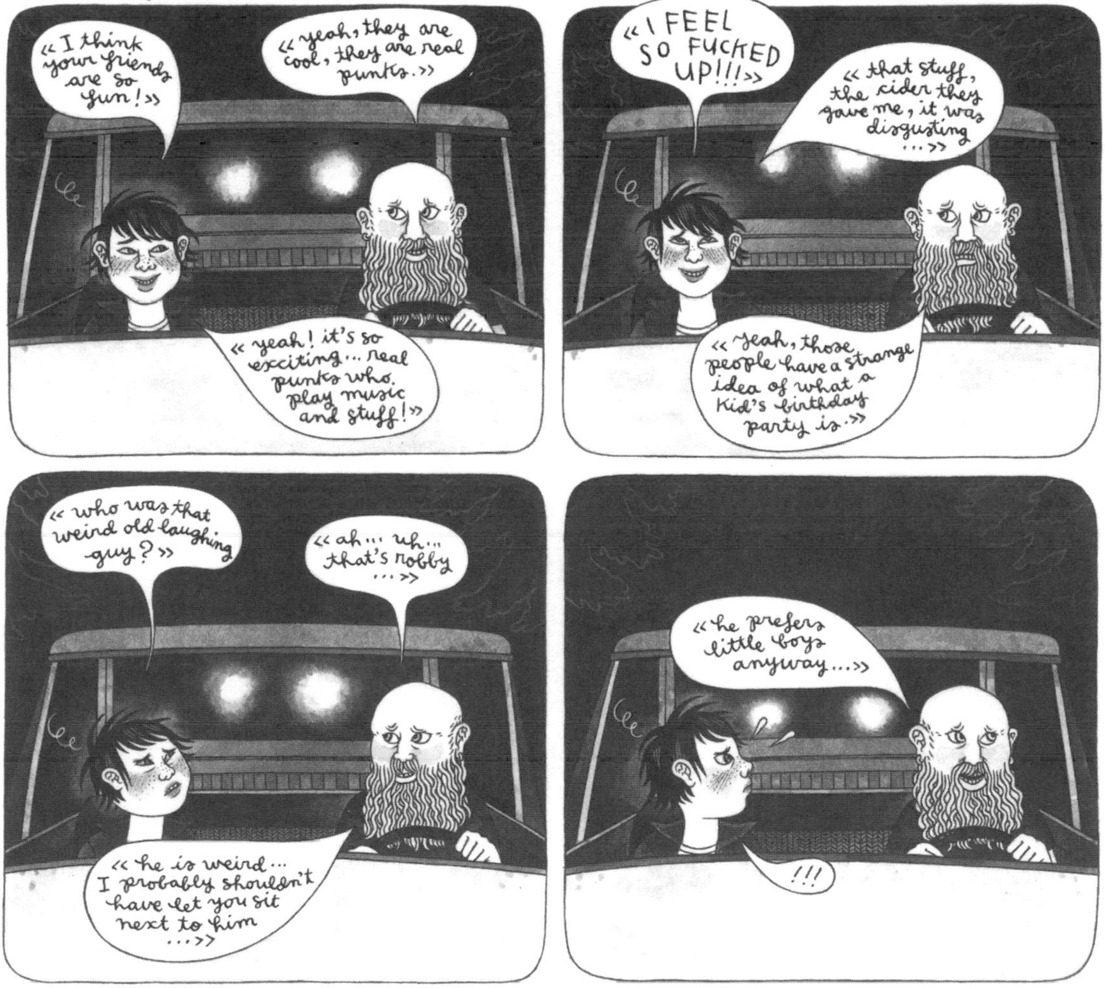
« I think your friends are so fun! »
« yeah, they are cool, they are real punks. »
« yeah! it's so exciting... real punks who play music and stuff! »
« I FEEL SO FUCKED UP!!! »
« that stuff, the cider they gave me, it was disgusting ... »
« Yeah, those people have a strange idea of what a kid's birthday party is. »
« who was that weird old laughing guy? »
« ah... uh... that's robby ... »
« he is weird... I probably shouldn't have let you sit next to him ... »
« he prefers little boys anyway... »
!!!

pcp.

I go to see punk bands play with my friends. I snort PCP in the bathroom. This is a popular drug with many youths my age. I have been getting high on weekends regularly, even when my friends are sober. One night my nose starts to bleed, then I start vomiting. I am not sure of what happens next. I am too out of it.

I am going to fail my math class...

my mom is going to kill me...

PASSED OUT UNDER THE TABLE.

ughh...

are you not sick?

no.

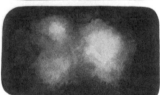

I move about the room in mysterious ways. Some friends lift me onto a chair. They are not pleased with me. I vomit again.

I go home. I forgot my keys. I sit and wait in the snow. Amère and Amer return from a party a little bit later. Amer pushes me with the tip of his toe.

I HAD COME HERE FOR THE MUSIC, BUT NOW...

I AM A HOLE.

goodbye.

what's the big idea?

I forgot my keys...

who are you talking to?

your daughter.

goglu, I won't let you go out anymore if you come back hungover like this...

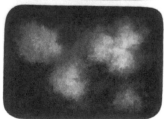

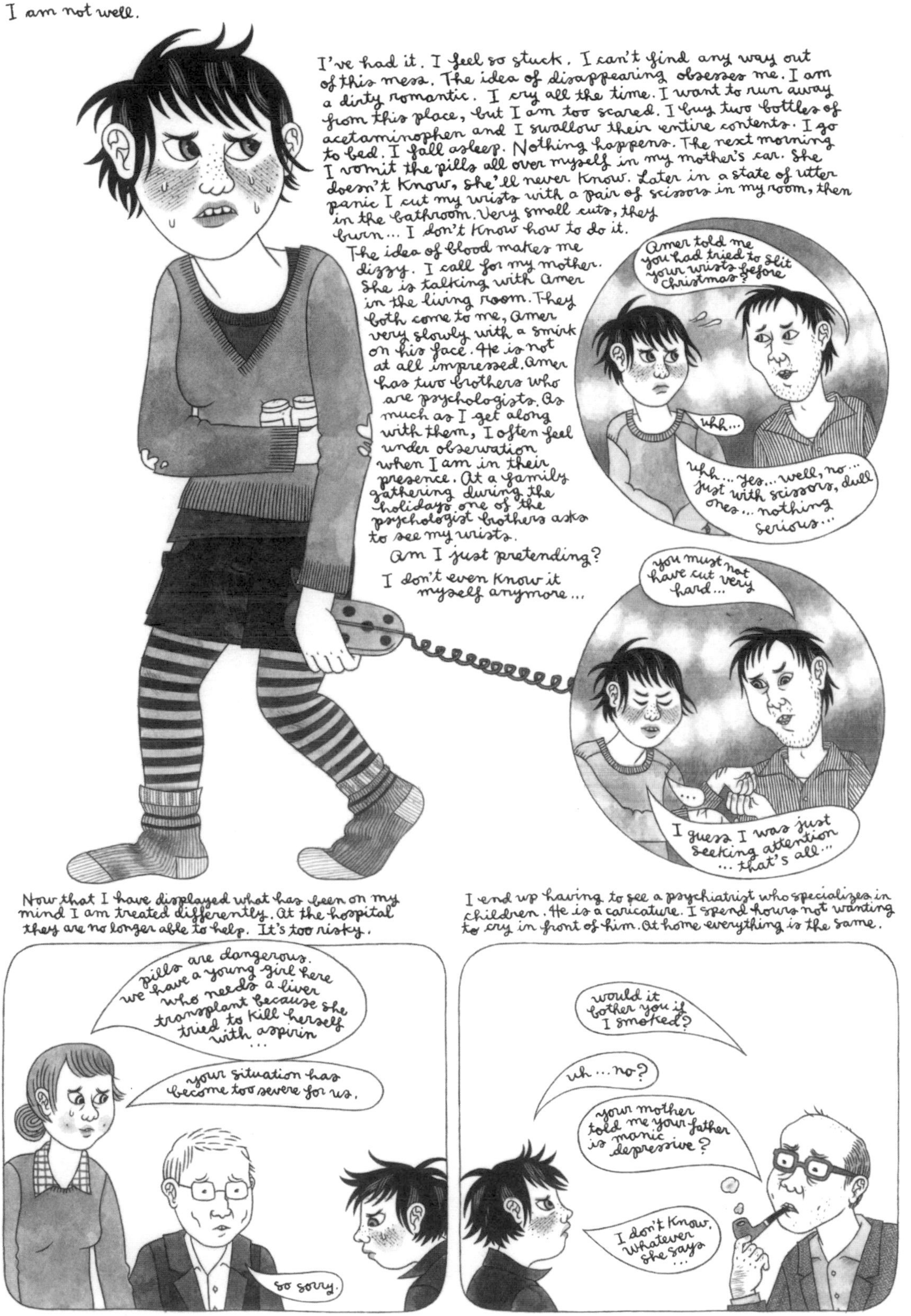
I am not well.
I've had it. I feel so stuck. I can't find any way out of this mess. The idea of disappearing obsesses me. I am a dirty romantic. I cry all the time. I want to run away from this place, but I am too scared. I buy two bottles of acetaminophen and I swallow their entire contents. I go to bed. I fall asleep. Nothing happens. The next morning I vomit the pills all over myself in my mother's car. She doesn't know, she'll never know. Later in a state of utter panic I cut my wrists with a pair of scissors in my room, then in the bathroom. Very small cuts, they burn... I don't know how to do it.
The idea of blood makes me dizzy. I call for my mother. She is talking with Amer in the living room. They both come to me, Amer very slowly with a smirk on his face. He is not at all impressed. Amer has two brothers who are psychologists. As much as I get along with them, I often feel under observation when I am in their presence. At a family gathering during the holidays one of the psychologist brothers asks to see my wrists.
Am I just pretending?
I don't even know it myself anymore...
Amer told me you had tried to slit your wrists before Christmas?
uhh...
uhh... yes... well, no... just with scissors, dull ones... nothing serious...
you must not have cut very hard...
...
I guess I was just seeking attention ... that's all...
Now that I have displayed what has been on my mind I am treated differently. At the hospital they are no longer able to help. It's too risky.
pills are dangerous. we have a young girl here who needs a liver transplant because she tried to kill herself with aspirin ...
your situation has become too severe for us.
so sorry.
I end up having to see a psychiatrist who specializes in children. He is a caricature. I spend hours not wanting to cry in front of him. At home everything is the same.
would it bother you if I smoked?
uh... no?
your mother told me your father is manic depressive?
I don't know. Whatever she says ...

in love.

He and I make a fort with blankets. We draw inside of it and do other things which aren't too serious but I still want to keep them private.

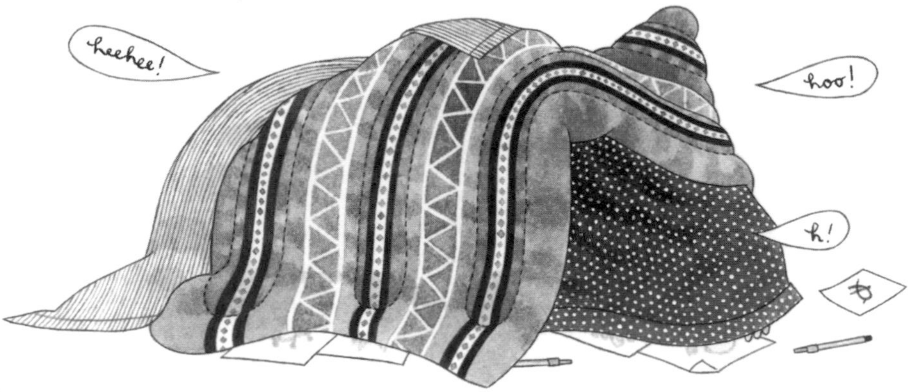
heehee!
hoo!
h!

I hate it when my mother tells me the boys I hang out with are handsome. It embarrasses me. I also don't like when she points out that they smell or have pimples. It makes me uneasy.

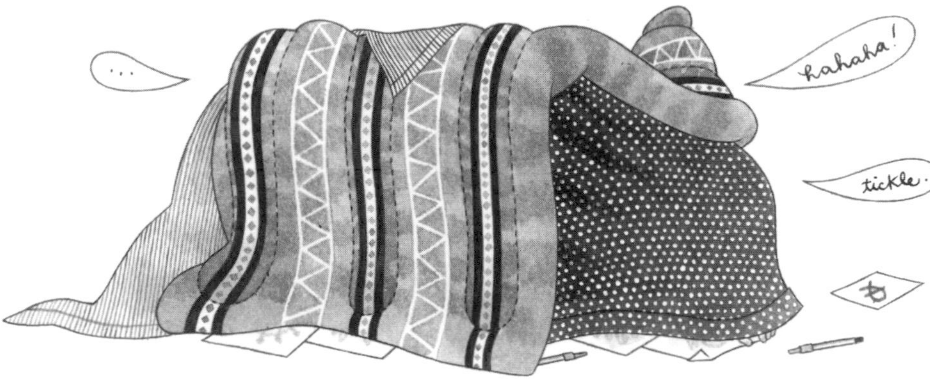
...
hahaha!
tickle.

I do not wish to know what Amère thinks of the boys I love.

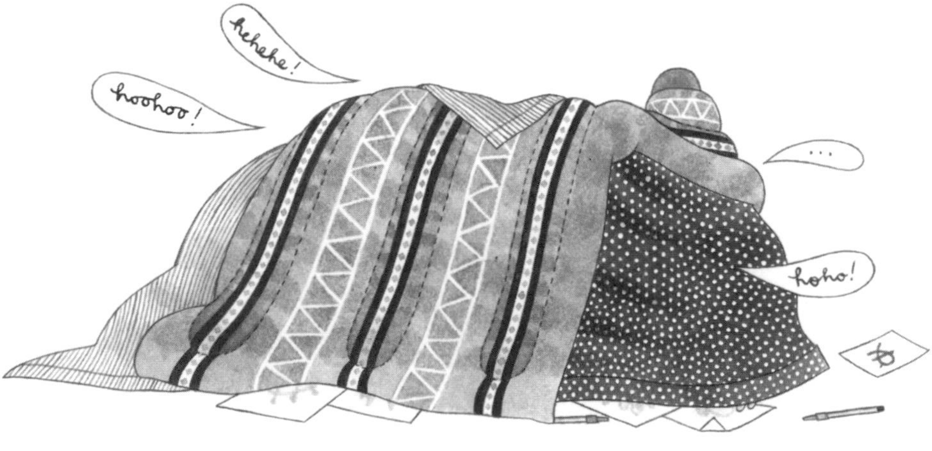
hehehe!
hoohoo!
...
hoho!

Venezuela.

Amer goes to Venezuela for his winter vacation, the second year in a row. My mother stays behind to take care of me and also because she cannot afford this type of extravagance. Since the last few months have been difficult, she lets me have friends over in secret.

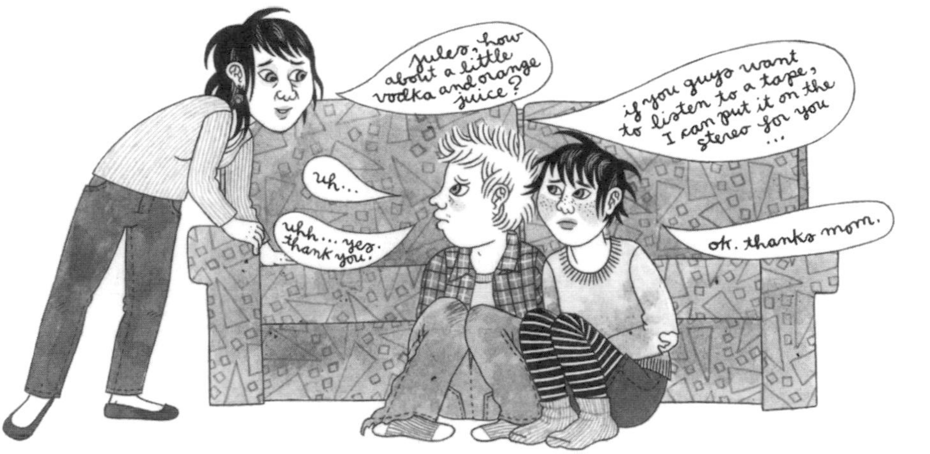

Jules, how about a little vodka and orange juice?
uh...
uhh... yes. thank you.
if you guys want to listen to a tape, I can put it on the stereo for you ...
ok. thanks mom.

My other friends came yesterday. I can't tell Amer about it. He would get angry. Jules is spending the night; him in the basement, me in my room. My mother tried her best to make my friends feel welcome. Tonight she is sad and drunk...

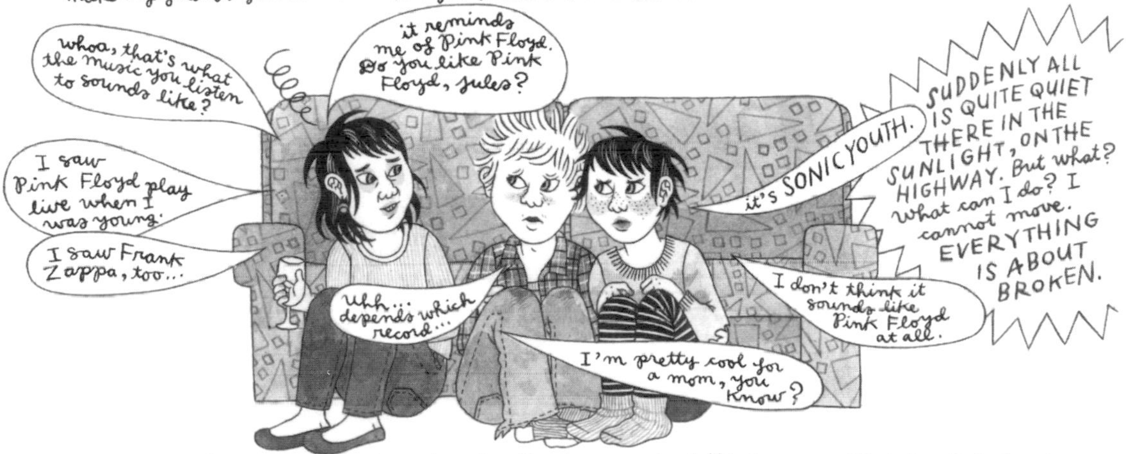

whoa, that's what the music you listen to sounds like?
it reminds me of Pink Floyd. Do you like Pink Floyd, Jules?
I saw Pink Floyd play live when I was young.
I saw Frank Zappa, too...
uhh... depends which record...
it's SONIC YOUTH.
SUDDENLY ALL IS QUITE QUIET THERE IN THE SUNLIGHT, ON THE HIGHWAY. But what? What can I do? I cannot move. EVERYTHING IS ABOUT BROKEN.
I don't think it sounds like Pink Floyd at all.
I'm pretty cool for a mom, you know?

When my mother is off to bed I stay in the basement a little longer with Jules. I feel red. The anger in me is rising... Why did Amère have to get drunk tonight? I can tell that Jules is uncomfortable. I do not know what to say. I pout. My mother throws up. We hear everything.

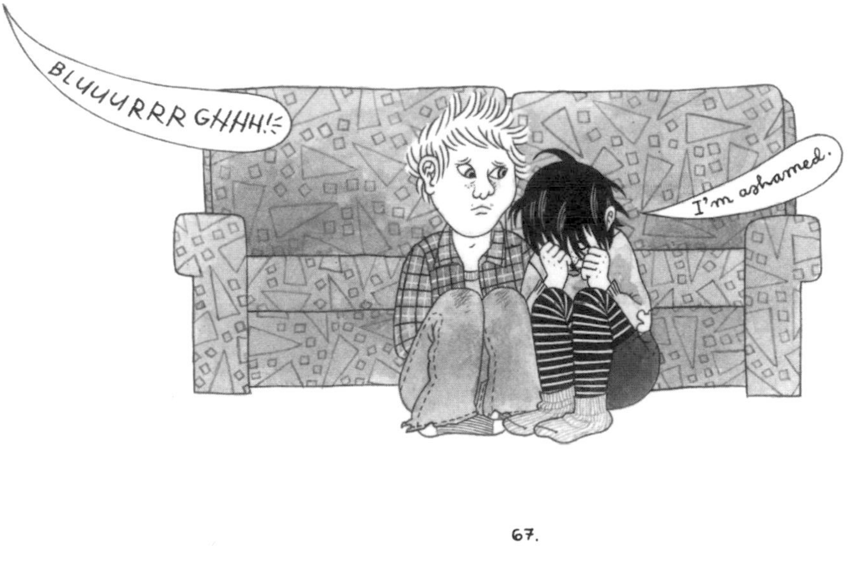

BLUUURRRGHHH!
I'm ashamed.

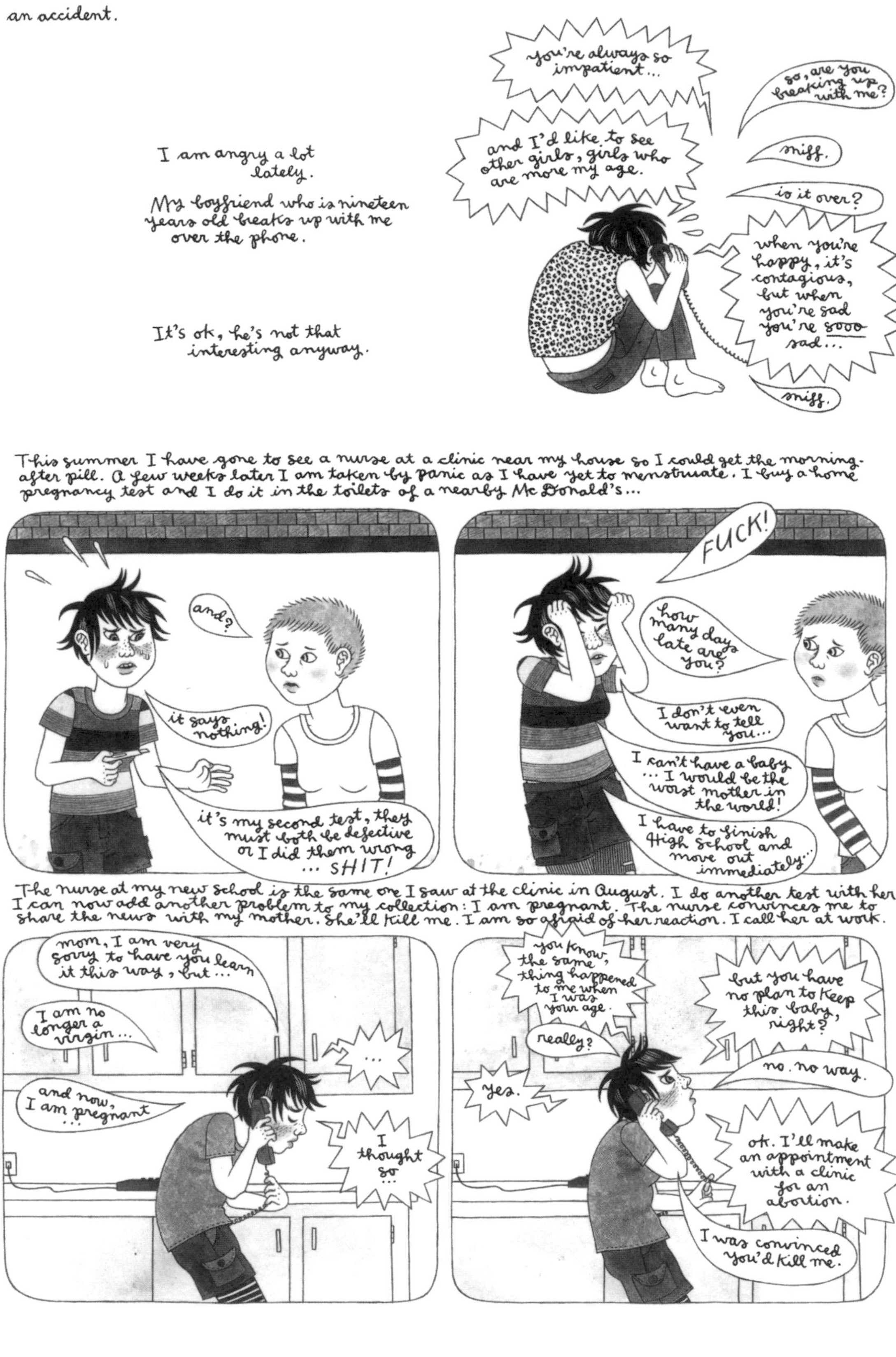
an accident.
I am angry a lot lately.
My boyfriend who is nineteen years old breaks up with me over the phone.
It's ok, he's not that interesting anyway.
you're always so impatient...
and I'd like to see other girls, girls who are more my age.
so, are you breaking up with me?
sniff.
is it over?
when you're happy, it's contagious, but when you're sad you're sooo sad...
sniff.
This summer I have gone to see a nurse at a clinic near my house so I could get the morning-after pill. A few weeks later I am taken by panic as I have yet to menstruate. I buy a home pregnancy test and I do it in the toilets of a nearby McDonald's...
and?
it says nothing!
it's my second test, they must both be defective or I did them wrong ... SHIT!
FUCK!
how many days late are you?
I don't even want to tell you...
I can't have a baby ... I would be the worst mother in the world!
I have to finish High School and move out immediately...
The nurse at my new school is the same one I saw at the clinic in August. I do another test with her. I can now add another problem to my collection: I am pregnant. The nurse convinces me to share the news with my mother. She'll kill me. I am so afraid of her reaction. I call her at work.
mom, I am very sorry to have you learn it this way, but...
I am no longer a virgin...
...
and now, I am pregnant...
I thought so...
you know, the same thing happened to me when I was your age.
really?
yes.
but you have no plan to keep this baby, right?
no. no way.
ok. I'll make an appointment with a clinic for an abortion.
I was convinced you'd kill me.

At the clinic I am the only girl accompanied by her mother. The other girls have come with a friend, except for one girl who is here with her boyfriend. In the waiting room everyone is nervous and silent but this boy can't hold it in any longer. A nurse asks him to calm down.

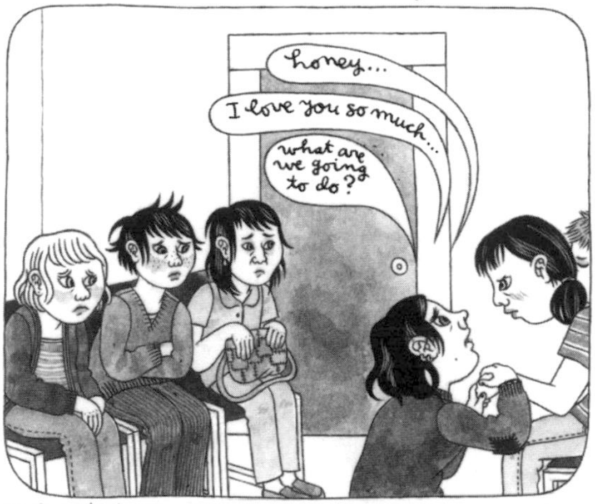
honey...
I love you so much...
what are we going to do?

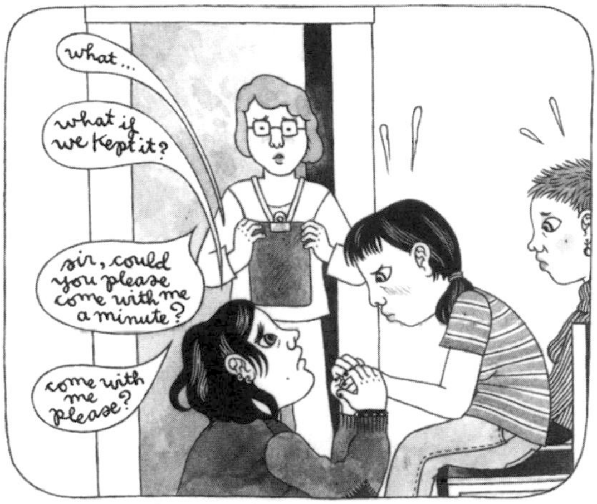
what...
what if we kept it?
sir, could you please come with me a minute?
come with me please?

I faint right after the abortion. That's my style. The nurses slap my face repeatedly. Once I am able to get up and walk I thank everyone. I feel relief like never before in my life. I feel liberated, even though I am vomiting everywhere...

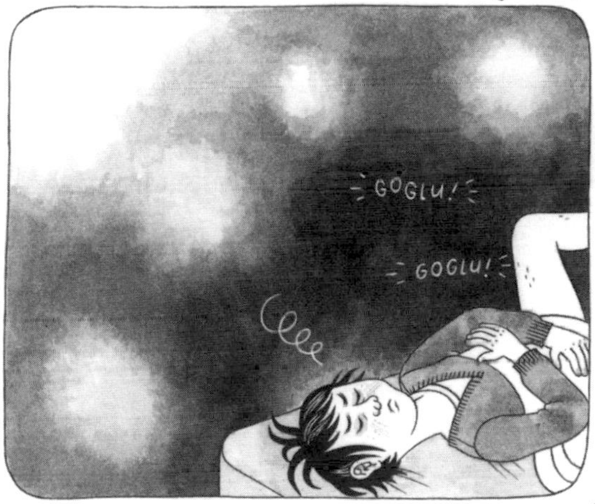
GOGLU!
GOGLU!

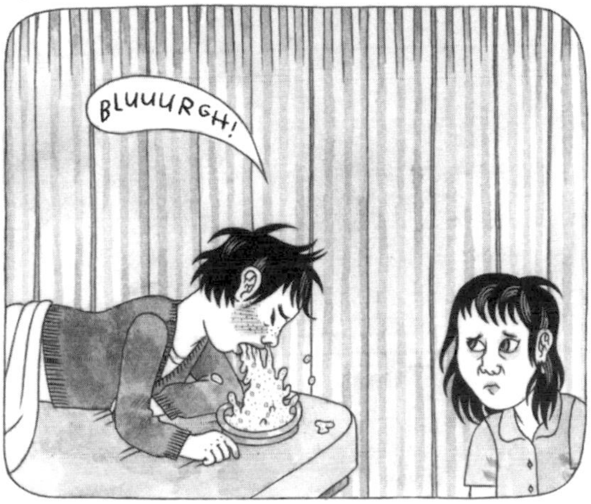
BLUUURGH!

Amère looks after me, she mothers me like she hasn't in years. Today our conflicts are put aside, my mother and I together for the same cause: I will not spend the rest of my seventeenth year awaiting a child. I have my whole life ahead of me. I have learned from my mistakes.

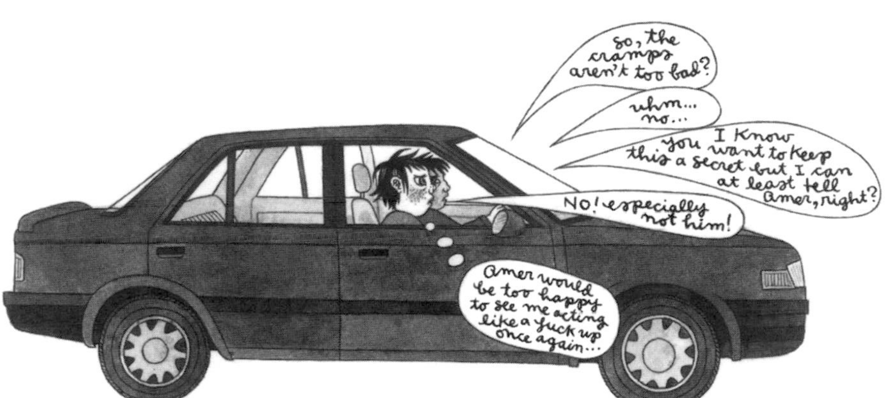
so, the cramps aren't too bad?
uhm... no...
I know you want to keep this a secret but I can at least tell Amer, right?
No! especially not him!
Amer would be too happy to see me acting like a fuck up once again...

hysteria.

I finish my last year of High School beautifully. I find work and I save money in order to move out with a friend in Montréal. We search for an apartment for a few weeks. Amer and Amère know that I am getting ready to leave. They even give me some dishes.

Once we find the perfect place, Amère refuses to help me sign the lease. I am still a minor after all.

I can't stand it anymore.

I ask my father about moving in with him and Sablée.

The weeks preceding my departure are pure insanity.

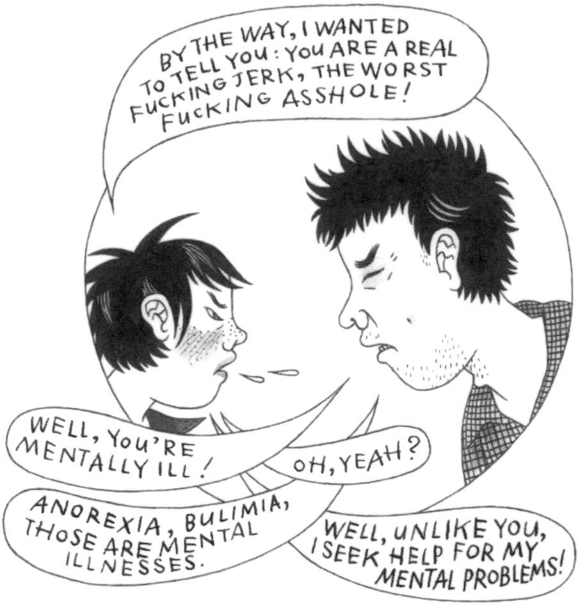

BY THE WAY, I WANTED TO TELL YOU: YOU ARE A REAL FUCKING JERK, THE WORST FUCKING ASSHOLE!
WELL, YOU'RE MENTALLY ILL!
OH, YEAH?
ANOREXIA, BULIMIA, THOSE ARE MENTAL ILLNESSES.
WELL, UNLIKE YOU, I SEEK HELP FOR MY MENTAL PROBLEMS!

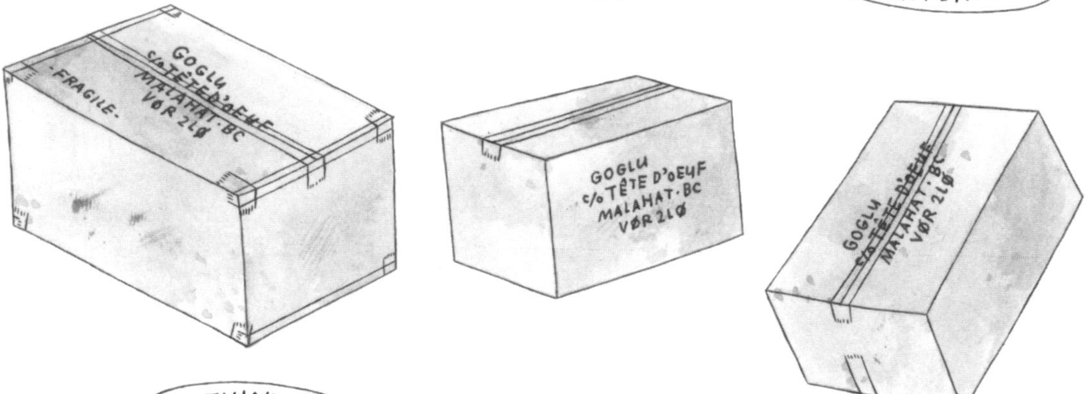

GOGLU C/O TÊTE D'OEUF MALAHAT · BC VØR 2LØ
·FRAGILE·
GOGLU C/O TÊTE D'OEUF MALAHAT · BC VØR 2LØ
GOGLU C/O TÊTE D'OEUF MALAHAT · BC VØR 2LØ

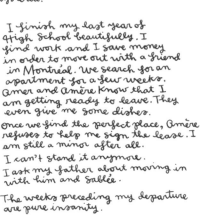

As she drives me to the airport my mother is overcome by guilt and explodes. She is shaking, there are cars everywhere. I do not want to miss my plane and I really don't want to get in an accident. A few days ago I told her I thought her head was empty.

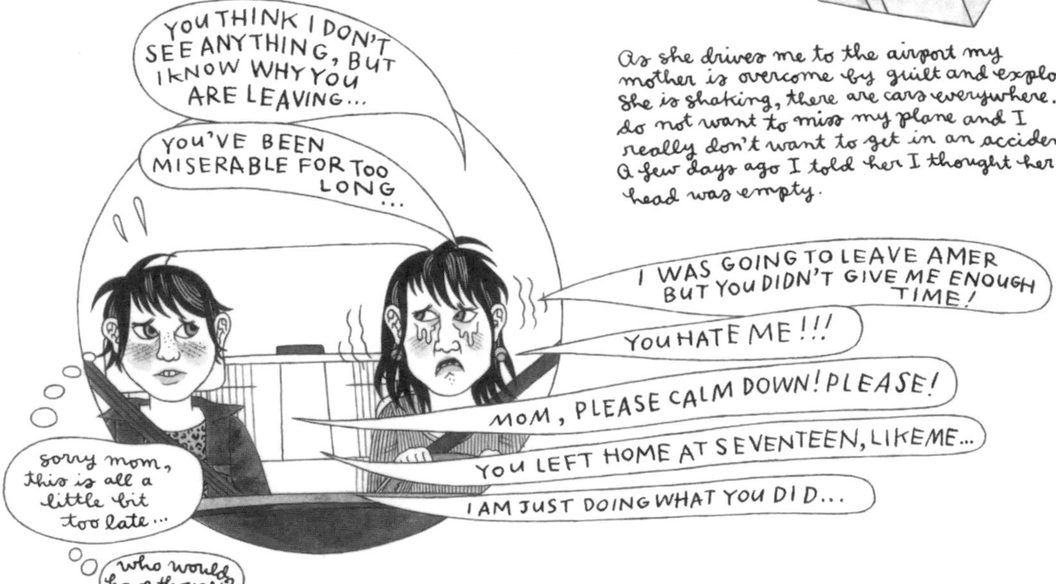

YOU THINK I DON'T SEE ANYTHING, BUT I KNOW WHY YOU ARE LEAVING...
YOU'VE BEEN MISERABLE FOR TOO LONG...
I WAS GOING TO LEAVE AMER BUT YOU DIDN'T GIVE ME ENOUGH TIME!
YOU HATE ME!!!
MOM, PLEASE CALM DOWN! PLEASE!
YOU LEFT HOME AT SEVENTEEN, LIKE ME...
I AM JUST DOING WHAT YOU DID...
sorry mom, this is all a little bit too late...
who would have thought?

I arrive in Victoria.

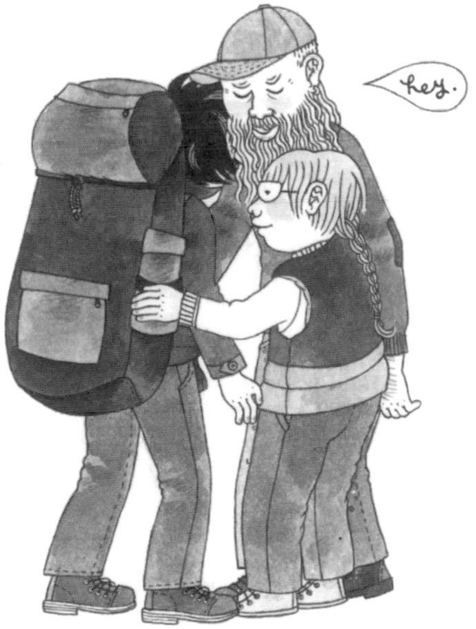
hey.

cabin.

I live out in the woods with my father and Sablée from the month of October till the month of May.

My father has built a log cabin for me. In it I sleep during the day and draw at night.

The closest village is an hour away on foot.

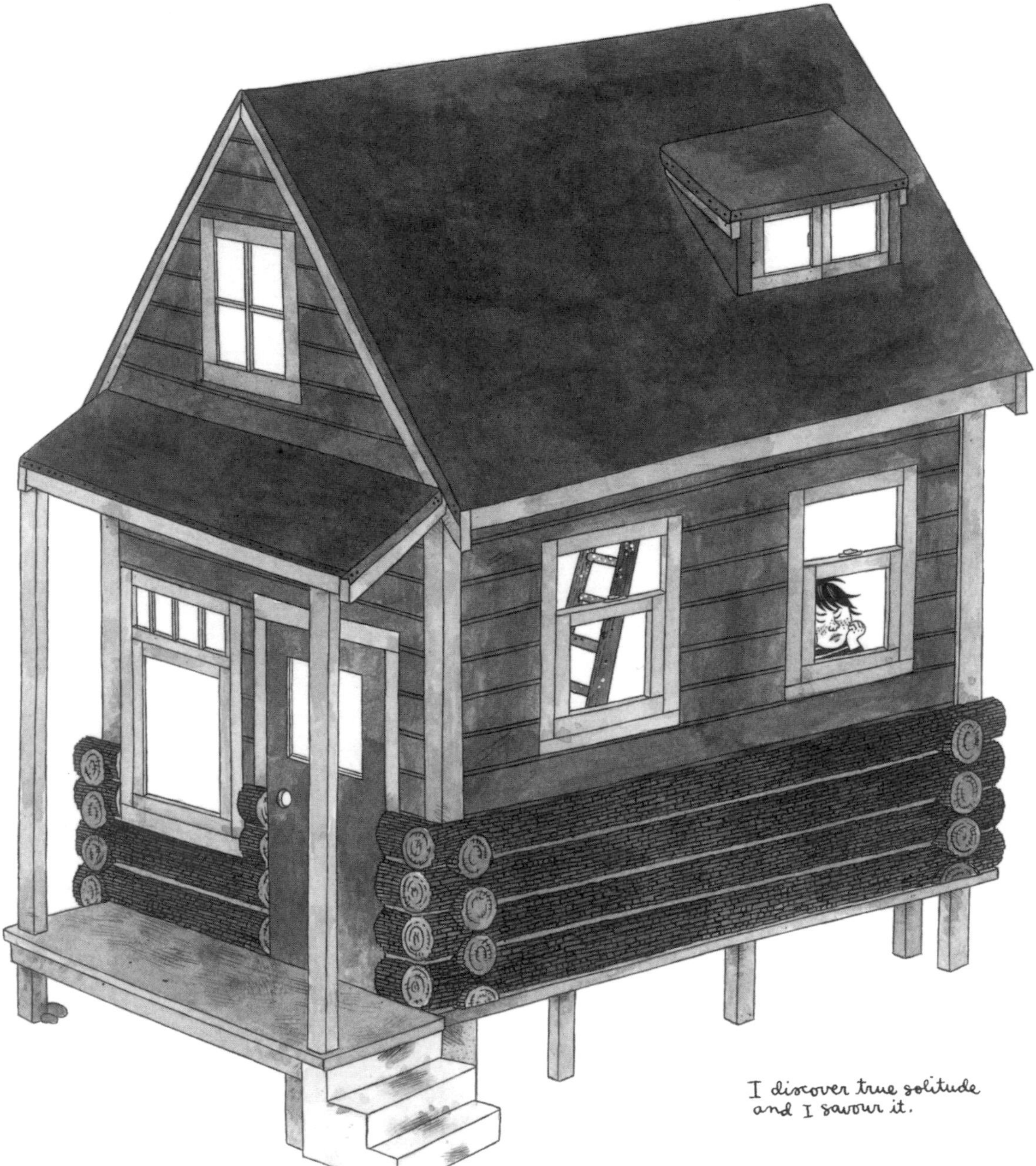

I discover true solitude and I savour it.

It seems as though by coming to live here I have left behind a parallel story that shapes and distorts itself on its own.

Before, I was more often aggressive, I was more often mean, more bitter.

I am no longer there to participate in it, or to defend myself.

It's because I am not really like a lot of other people.

Tête d'Oeuf says I should be proud of it.

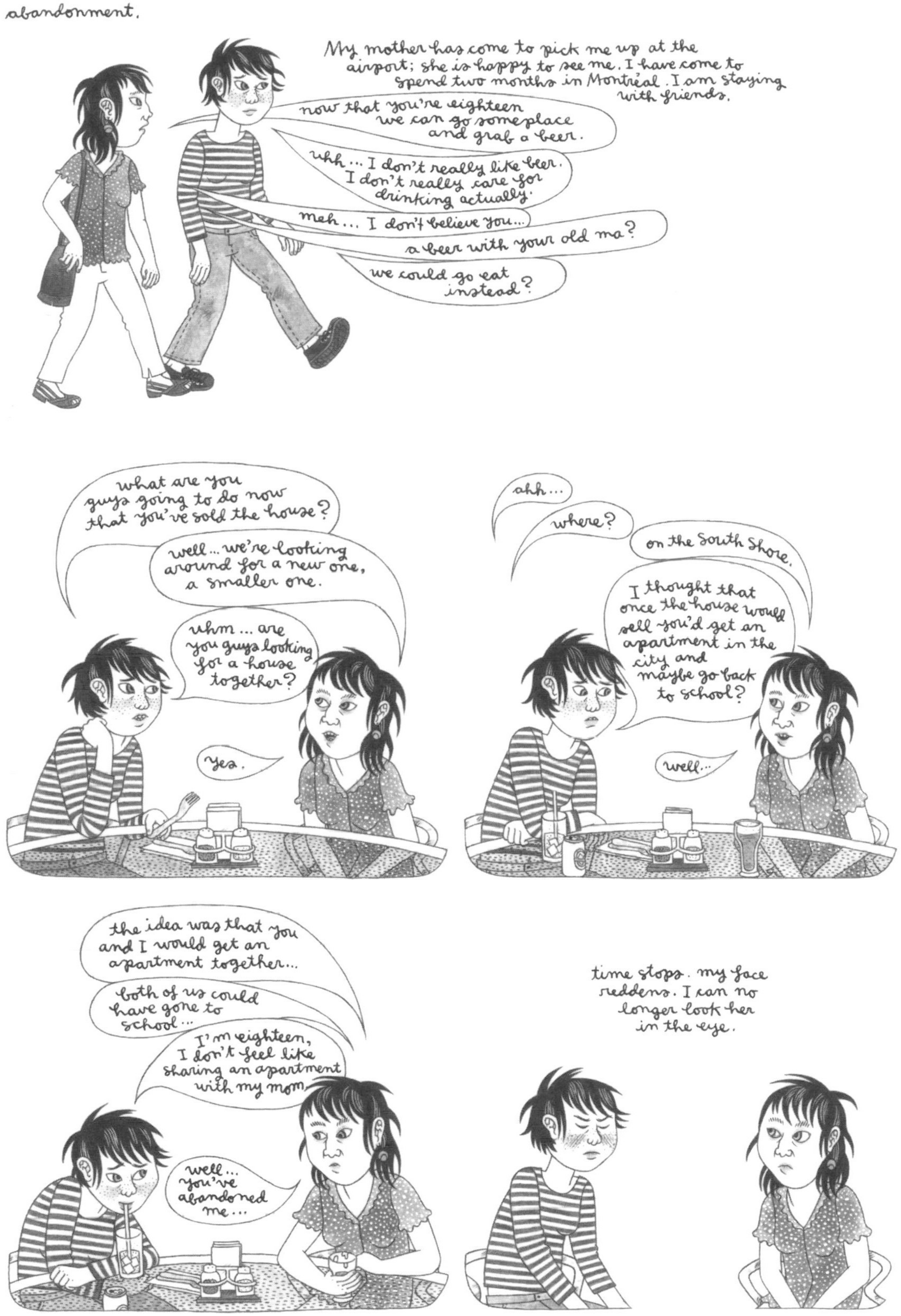
abandonment.
My mother has come to pick me up at the airport; she is happy to see me. I have come to spend two months in Montréal. I am staying with friends.
now that you're eighteen we can go someplace and grab a beer.
uhh ... I don't really like beer. I don't really care for drinking actually.
meh ... I don't believe you...
a beer with your old ma?
we could go eat instead?
what are you guys going to do now that you've sold the house?
well... we're looking around for a new one, a smaller one.
uhm ... are you guys looking for a house together?
yes.
ahh...
where?
on the South Shore.
I thought that once the house would sell you'd get an apartment in the city and maybe go back to school?
well...
the idea was that you and I would get an apartment together...
both of us could have gone to school...
I'm eighteen, I don't feel like sharing an apartment with my mom.
well... you've abandoned me...
time stops. my face reddens. I can no longer look her in the eye.

I can do whatever I want.

GENEVIÈVE CASTRÉE was born in Québec in 1981.
She has been drawing since the age of two.
Castrée lives and works in the Pacific-Northwest,
where she makes visual art, sculpts small objects,
and collects stamps. She also plays music under the
name "Ô PAON".